FACING SOUTHWEST

PHOTOGRAPHY BY ROBERT RECK

W. W. Norton & Company   New York • London

Facing Southwest

THE LIFE & HOUSES OF JOHN GAW MEEM

CHRIS WILSON

Copyright © 2001 by W. W. Norton & Company, Inc.

Photographs copyright © 2001 by Robert Reck

Printed in the United States of America

First published as a Norton paperback 2005

For information about permission to reproduce selections from this book, write to Permissions, W. W. Norton & Company, Inc., 500 Fifth Avenue, New York, NY 10110

The text of this book is composed in Monotype Walbaum

With the display set in Luna and FF Eureka Sans

Separations by Bright Arts Graphics

Manufacturing by KHL Printing

Book design by Kristina Kachele

Supplemental drawings by George Clayton Pearl

Production manager: Leeann Graham

Frontispiece: Photo by Robert Reck

Library of Congress Cataloging-in-Publication Data

Wilson, Chris, 1951 Dec. 23–

Facing Southwest : the life and houses of John Gaw Meem / Christopher Wilson ; photography by Robert Reck.

p. cm.

Includes bibliographical references and index.

ISBN 0-393-73067-0

1. Meem, John Gaw, 1894—Criticism and interpretation.

2. Architecture—Southwest, New—20th century.

3. Architecture, Domestic—Southwest, New.

I. Reck, Robert, 1945–

II. Title.

NA737.M438 W55 2001

728'.092—dc21

0-393-73175-8 (pbk.)   2001031488

W. W. Norton & Company, Inc., 500 Fifth Avenue, New York, N.Y. 10110

www.wwnorton.com

W. W. Norton & Company Ltd., Castle House, 75/76 Wells Street, London W1T 3QT

0 9 8 7 6 5 4 3 2 1

CONTENTS

FACING SOUTHWEST

PART I

FACING SOUTHWEST

I n the late 1920s, near the beginning of his career, John Gaw Meem sometimes met prospective clients at La Fonda, the Spanish-Pueblo–style hotel at the southeast corner of the old Santa Fe plaza. Lunch and afternoon tea were served in a cloistered patio lined by Spanish *portales*—open porches with log posts and heavy carved wooden brackets; the patio was added in 1927 and designed by Meem himself. His formal demeanor and soft-spoken, attentive manner won over many clients. Gentle, modest, and professional, with refined manners, an air of authority, and the ability to pour on the charm—these are the words used to describe Meem today by those who knew him.

As Mr. and Mrs. Ferdinand Koch described their dream house at such a conference in August 1928, Meem jotted this concise list:

Garage (2 car)	Living room	Nursery
Rear entry (refrig)	Recess bookcase	Walls Hollow tile
Kitchen (elec range)	Fireplace	Stucco adobe color
Breakfast room (4)	Master Bedroom	Basement Coal & boiler steam
Dining room	Large closet or 2 small	Storage & oil.[1]
	Sleeping porch	

Occasionally, Meem proceeded to rough out a floor plan on a piece of hotel stationery, but more often the conference was soon adjourned to visit the building site.

Dressed in his customary brown tweed suit and tie, round wire-rimmed glasses and broad-brimmed Borsalino, Meem walked the foothills around Santa Fe with the Steadmans, McCormicks, and Chases of Chicago; Amelia Hollenback of Brooklyn; the Hownells of Bryn Mawr, Pennsylvania; the Proctors of Winter Park, Florida; and the Carlisles of South Bend, Indiana; as well as Jesse Nusbaum, Ruth Heflin, and other Santa Fe residents.[2] For the newcomers at least, site visits generally occurred at the end of a summer vacation, or following an enchanting Santa Fe Fiesta in early September. Winding through juniper and bushy piñon pine on rocky hillsides, Meem and his clients sought a site that might be inexpensively leveled to receive a house and could also command panoramic landscape views.

At that time of year, the aspen-covered flanks of the Sangre de Cristo Mountains to the north begin to show their fall colors. Sixty miles to the south, the bulky Sandias are seen sprawling across the broad desert floor, while to the west, on the far side of the Rio Grande, the late afternoon sun raking the Jemez Mountains transforms them into an immense backdrop of layered, rugged profiles. If Meem and his clients lingered while the sun floated down to the western horizon, the aspens to the north glowed yellow, then golden as if on fire. Then, as now, the experience of this vast, illuminated landscape stretching out fifty miles in three directions is one of the chief attractions of Santa Fe. The nineteenth-century Romantics had a term for such a transfiguring experience of grandeur and awe—they called it the Sublime. Capturing this landscape experience became a primary imperative of Meem's residential commissions.

During these years, John Gaw Meem brought Santa Fe style to maturity. By calming the overly picturesque details and compositions of the style as practiced before his arrival in 1920, and instead emphasizing the sculptural massiveness of adobe, Meem imbued Santa Fe style with a dignified monumentality. His house plans drew elements from the local Spanish and Pueblo vernaculars, and from the axial formality of Beaux-Arts design. But under the romantic aesthetic, Meem also relaxed and opened his houses out to commanding landscape views and the brilliant light and winter warmth of the Southwestern sun.

Many well-designed houses of a certain age are reverently—sometimes apocryphally—attributed to Meem in and around Santa Fe, the way other houses are attributed to Bernard Maybeck in Berkeley, George Washington Smith in Santa Barbara, Wallace Neff in the Los Angeles area, Irving Gill in San Diego, Addison Mizner in Palm Beach, and Frank Lloyd Wright in Chicago. This is the architectural equivalent of "Washington slept here," revealing the desire for a direct connection to the mythic touchstones of regional architectural traditions.

NOTE: Unless otherwise noted, all illustrated buildings are designed by Meem's firm and located in Santa Fe.

FORMATIVE EXPERIENCES

John Gaw Meem was the fourth to bear that name. The first was a third-generation American of Dutch and Polish German ancestry, who settled in the Shenandoah Valley of western Virginia in 1839. A long line of Meem men attended the Virginia Military Institute (VMI); most majored in civil engineering. Meem's grandfather, the second John Gaw Meem, worked on the design of the first rail line in Brazil, then returned to serve as a colonel in the Confederate army, before settling into a career as a supervising architect with the U.S. Treasury Department in Washington, DC.

Meem's father, the third John Gaw Meem, also majored in engineering at VMI, but, amid one of the many religious awakenings that swept through nineteenth-century America, felt a divine call to the ministry. He volunteered to be an Episcopal missionary in 1891 and, after two years building his new congregation in the southern Brazilian coastal town of Pelotas, married a young German-Brazilian woman named Elsa Upton Krischke. Pelotas and its sister city, the port of Rio Grande, where she was raised, controlled trade in the cattle-ranching, tall grass pampas of southern Brazil. Of mixed German, American, and Portuguese ancestry, Krischke came from a group of mercantile families who felt themselves to be loyal Brazilians. A demure seventeen when she married the earnest, twenty-nine-year-old missionary, she gave birth to their first child, John Gaw Meem IV, at the end of 1894.

Young Meem grew up speaking Portuguese with his mother and English with his father, who also tutored him in German. Although he was raised to think of himself as American, Meem also unavoidably acquired the nonverbal body language, spatial patterns, and rhythms of social interaction from his mother and the surrounding community. On the plazas of Pelotas for evening promenade, or in the formal entry halls and parlors of its elegant town houses, Meem learned the elaborate etiquette of a hierarchical society that emphasized formality and mutual respect in relations among social classes,

Meem family at Mt. Airy, the family ancestral home in the Shenandoah Valley of Virginia (about 1896). Back: James L. Meem, Julia H. Meem. Middle: Reverend J. G. Meem III, Elsa Krischke Meem, J. G. Meem II, Stephen H. Meem. On lap: Nancy "Nanita" Cowan Meem, J. G. Meem IV. Seated: Catherine D. Meem, James ("Uncle Jim") Meem.

The third, fourth, and second John Gaw Meem.

John Gaw Meem IV with his mother and sisters Nanita and Lucy.

Two-story Meem family home in Pelotas, Brazil.

Main plaza in Pelotas, Brazil. (Photo by John Wirth, 1964)

Episcopalian Church in Pelotas, Brazil, designed by John Gaw Meem III
(1908). (John Wirth, 1964)

generations, and the sexes. As he entered his teens, the city's French-influenced Renaissance Revival buildings were joined by one contrasting accent—a substantial Gothic Revival church designed by his father.[3]

Then, in the summer of 1910, Meem, not quite sixteen, boarded a freighter bound for the United States to enroll at VMI. In his bag were copies of the poems of Olavo Bilac, and Euclydes da Cunha's *Os Sertões*—the Brazilian national epic, a book he would later carry to Santa Fe. Looking back in retirement over his architectural career, Meem told the *VMI Alumni Review*, "I am sure that the discipline I learned at VMI has been immensely helpful to me." However American

Cadets leaving the parade grounds, Virginia Military Institute (about 1912).

Meem as officer of the day overseeing young sentinel, VMI (1911).

Robert Colhoun, Meem, Phyllis Harding, and Stella Colhoun at Allegheny Springs resort (1913).

Elevated subway construction, New York (about 1915).

(From Meem family album.)

he may have felt in Pelotas, Meem's accented English and slight build made him the target of merciless hazing—one beating ended with a broomstick broken over his back. His closest school friend, Fritz Krantel, was also from Brazil. At VMI, as in Pelotas, Meem remained in part an outsider.[4]

After receiving a B.S. in engineering at age nineteen in 1914, Meem joined his uncle James C. Meem's Underpinning and Foundation Company in New York, where young Meem worked for two years on the design of Manhattan subway and elevated rail lines. As his engineering expertise matured, he also observed an office that operated under emerging scientific management techniques and a rhetoric of professional expertise. During World War I, Meem was commissioned a captain in the U.S. Army and commanded a battalion that trained green recruits in Iowa.

At the close of the war, Meem was stricken by the 1918 influenza, an epidemic that mysteriously killed more young adults than elders. After recovering, he decided to rejoin his family, which had moved to Rio de Janeiro during his absence. A position as credit manager for National City Bank of New York in Rio promised a career in international finance. But after only a few months in Brazil, he was diagnosed with tuberculosis. The bank, which would pay for his treatment, recalled him to New York. (In time, Meem's younger brother, James, attended VMI, became a banker, and settled in the United States, but their mother and three sisters, Nancy (Nanita), Lucy, and Elsa, remained in Brazil after their missionary father died in 1924.)

In those days, TB was often, though not always, fatal, and such a diagnosis occasioned a response similar to cancer or HIV today. Until the discovery of an antibiotic treatment in 1943, any chance of recovery from TB depended on complete rest in a sanitarium, which is what the bank's doctor in New York prescribed. As Meem recalled in later years, he walked despondently down Fifth Avenue until photos of the desert Southwest and adobe architecture on display in the windows of a Santa Fe Railway ticket office caught his eye. His physician had mentioned Santa Fe as one place to take the cure, and he decided on the spot to go.[5]

When a gaunt, twenty-five-year-old John Meem stepped off the train in early 1920, Santa Fe was in the midst of a major architectural makeover. After the main Chicago-to-Los Angeles rail line bypassed the city in 1880, the county government had to pay for the construction of a connecting spur line. Even as the business community sought to make Santa Fe into a modern

city of Italianate business blocks and French Second Empire–style civic buildings, the disadvantage of being off the main rail line caused the city's economy to slump and its population to begin a steady thirty-year decline. In 1912, local business boosters and the staff of the new Museum of New Mexico devised a plan to revive the city's economy through the development of tourism. They proposed remaking the now much-Americanized city in the Santa Fe style—a revival based equally on remaining Spanish- and Mexican-era buildings and nearby Pueblo villages. The Palace of the Governors on the north side of the plaza was restored in 1913, a handsome Fine Arts museum patterned after the adobe missions appeared in 1916, and, when Meem arrived in 1920, four major Santa Fe–style buildings were under construction. The local firm of Rapp, Rapp & Hendrickson designed the best of the lot: the museum, La Fonda, and Meem's destination, the Sunmount Sanitarium. The style's leading proponent, the painter Carlos Vierra, was then erecting a house for himself to demonstrate the suitability of the revival style for residences.[6]

Taking its name from Sunmount Hill—Monte Sol—southeast of the city, the sanitarium was built on the side of a smaller hill. The ground-level entry of the building leads through a common room to a covered terrace fifteen feet above the desert floor, which commands a panorama stretching from nearby Monte Sol south and west to the distant Sandia Mountains. On arrival, Meem was admitted to the hospital wards on the upper floors, where patients slept on screened-in porches, regardless of the weather.

Hartford insurance executive and spare-time poet Wallace Stevens once enquired, "How

La Fonda Hotel, Santa Fe, designed by Rapp, Rapp & Hendrickson (1920).

does one stand/to behold the sublime?" Stevens plumbed as deeply as anyone into experiences of life in the industrial, commercial city—the world Meem knew from his time in New York but had left behind. Stevens wanted to know how we keep human awe for the grandeur and sacredness of existence alive in such a world. How, we might wonder, did John Meem feel the first morning he awoke on one of those screened-in porches with enough energy to notice the way the sun breaking around Sunmount casts long piñon shadows across the gravelly desert floor? And how did his stance in the world shift after he learned to trace the daily arch of the sun across the sky to its crimson and purple setting beyond the Jemez Mountains? The evidence of the buildings he later designed, and of the generous spirit he carried into the life of his adopted community, suggests he had learned how one stands to behold the sublime. Like so many of his fellow patients, John Meem not only regained his physical health, but he was also reborn psychologically facing southwest across Sunmount's sunbathed panorama.

The director of the Sunmount Sanitarium, Dr. Frank E. Mera, prescribed a standard regimen of rest, healthy diet, and nights on those open sleeping porches. Santa Fe's location at 7,000 ft (2133 m) offered the pure mountain air thought essential to the cure. Mera also sought to counter the depression that so often accompanied TB. His new Santa Fe–style building stood as a sun-soaked refuge from the rush and pollution of modern urban life. He also encouraged patients to cultivate their interests and made Sunmount an active community center for its blossoming art colony. Part sanitarium, part hotel, Sunmount's common room regularly hosted public talks by writer Mary Austin, poet Witter Bynner, archaeologists Edgar Lee Hewett and Sylvanus G. Morley, and other local notables. Vachel Lindsey and Carl Sandburg gave poetry readings, Robert Flaherty screened his groundbreaking documentary "Nanook of the North," and many guest speakers resided at Sunmount while in Santa Fe.

Aware of Meem's engineering background and original attraction to Santa Fe, Mera soon introduced him to Carlos Vierra. Son of a Portuguese-American fishing family near Monterey, California, Vierra shared the Portuguese language with Meem and soon fired him with his passion for Southwestern adobe architecture. Before long, Meem was propped up in his bed sketching the landscape. He also translated poems by the Brazilian Olavo Bilac, which were published in a small volume with the poetry of Ivor Winters, a friend and fellow Sunmount patient.[7]

Meem at Sunmount Sanitarium (1921).

opposite
Sunmount Sanitarium, showing sleeping porches (about 1920).

Lounge, Sunmount Sanitarium (about 1920).

Patient room and sleeping porch, Sunmount Sanitarium (about 1920). (From Meem Collection, New Mexico State Record Center.)

ARCHITECTURAL TRAINING

After a year and a half at the sanitarium, Dr. Mera pronounced Meem sufficiently recovered
to pursue an apprenticeship with leading Denver architects Fisher & Fisher. Like other major
firms across the country, they adhered to the Beaux-Arts design approach—named for the preeminent architecture school, the Ecole des Beaux-Arts in Paris. In addition to designing large
residences and public buildings, William, the older Fisher brother, was also the president of
the Architects' Small House Service, Mountain Bureau. Reasoning that most prospective
homeowners could not afford the cost of an architect, the Bureau specialized in standardized
plans for one- to three-bedroom houses. Their plans made the most of the limited resources of
middle-class families by specifying stock lumber and standard doors and windows; by devel-
oping compact, efficient arrangements of rooms that reduced corridors to a minimum by using
the rooms themselves for circulation; and by emphasizing efficient kitchens with built-in cabinets rather than pantries, and breakfast nooks instead of full dining rooms. Each plan employed textured brick or stucco and a few strategically placed details to evoke the American
Colonial, French Provincial, Italian, or Spanish Mission style.[8]

After working days over a drafting table for Fisher & Fisher, Meem attended an evening
architectural studio, the Atelier Denver. The Beaux-Arts Institute of Design in New York City
set the architectural curriculum for American universities and a network of independent ate-
liers, which were studios in rented space where practicing architects tutored beginners. The
younger brother, Arthur Fisher, had completed the Institute's program and taught in the
Atelier Denver. But the director and dominating force of Atelier Denver was thirty-seven-year-
old Burnham Hoyt, who had attracted national attention in the early 1910s as the most daring student in the history of the Institute; he would later distinguish himself as Colorado's
leading mid-century architect and as dean of the New York University architecture school.[9]

The Beaux-Arts Institute regularly distributed design problems for four levels of students;
these were a coordinated series of exercises based on the French system, but tempered by
American pragmatism. Students were urged to familiarize themselves with the requirements
of various building types, their typical rooms, and arrangements. They learned, for instance,
the standard rooms for a small town library, a railway terminal, or a city hall, and how architects had satisfied similar building programs in the past. Within a house or a particular building type, they needed to know the appropriate size and proportions for each room—those for
a master bedroom or the living room of a large country house, for a theater lobby, or for a
memorial chapel seating sixty. They were also encouraged to observe the movement of crowds
in public buildings and to absorb the designs of historic and recently completed buildings from
books and architectural journals. Above all, they learned to value historical precedent and conventional design solutions.[10]

The Beaux-Arts approach emphasized the use of symmetrical facades and floor plans derived largely from the classical formality of Greece, Rome, and the Italian Renaissance. By the 1920s, American Colonial and Greek Revival architecture and Spanish Colonial missions were also deemed worthy of study and emulation. Books on classical and Gothic architecture had begun to appear in the nineteenth century, and were joined by monographs on national and regional traditions as the number of titles and the lavishness of illustrations peaked in the 1920s. Just as an aspiring writer might commit a passage of the King James Bible, *Hamlet*, or Whitman's *Leaves of Grass* to memory, a Beaux-Arts student would pore over the writings of Vitruvius and Palladio, and more recent books with titles like *French Cathedrals, Monasteries and Abbeys*, and *The Domestic Architecture of the American Colonies*. Now and then tracing paper was laid over a favorite detail, and it was copied by hand as a way of committing it to memory. Just as the great European tradition became a subconscious reservoir of phrases and images that echoed in the cadences of a mature poet, the spaces, proportions, and details of classical buildings resonated in the designs of a great architect.

The Institute's program guided students in stages from the simplest to the most complex design problems, from the mastery of the proportions and detailing of a window to the composition of a facade, from the design of building floor plans to the organization of large complexes of buildings. In professional practice, Beaux-Arts architects reversed this sequence, working from broad issues to smallest details. First, bearing in mind all of the client's requirements and how earlier buildings had resolved similar building programs, the architect would sketch a number of possible solutions—in French, *parti*—schemes that efficiently accommodated the building's various functions. Such a plan would be intelligible to the public because of its symmetry and similarity to existing buildings of the type. Near the end of this plan development process, the architect began to study facade elevations and cross-sections through the major rooms to ensure that the plan would yield a pleasing exterior composition and properly proportioned spaces. After refining facade compositions, the architect finally turned to ornamental details and color schemes. At any step in the process, a book might be pulled from the office library to consider possible historic variations for the project at hand.

To the extent that architectural modernism shapes our attitudes today, this Beaux-Arts approach may strike us as imitative—as somehow false, dishonest, and lacking in creativity. The philosophy of Modernism, which rose against the Beaux Arts in the 1930s and swept it completely from the field after the Second World War, holds that a building should not only satisfy programmatic requirements—something the Beaux-Arts also sought—but should express these functions on its exterior and also reflect the spirit of the modern machine age. This exaltation of emerging industrial construction technologies, when combined with the particularities

AN ORANGERIE

of a site and building program, called for unique solutions, even the invention of totally new forms. The regime of compulsive innovation made heroes of architects who thumbed their noses at tradition. But for the Beaux-Arts designers, it was only common sense to begin each design from the hard-won lessons of previous generations of architects.

Under the Beaux-Arts Institute program, the best work from each school and atelier was sent to New York to be judged against students from all over the country. Six months into the program, Meem's design for the entrance to a Marine Museum won a First Mention—the highest award for a first-year project—and was chosen as one of four designs for publication in *American Architect* magazine. Although his health allowed him to complete only a third of the Institute's four-year program, Meem's subsequent career gave ample indications of his Beaux-Arts training and time with Fisher & Fisher. Meem remained committed throughout his career to the value of historic precedents and of time-tested solutions to recurrent design problems.[11]

EARLY PRACTICE

Sixteen months of sixteen-hour days proved too much for a constitution compromised by influenza and TB, and Meem returned to Sunmount in January 1924. Soon after, Dr. Mera made available a building on the sanitarium grounds, where Meem opened an architectural practice. (Fellow patient and accountant Cassius McCormick served as his partner and business manager until McCormick returned home to Chicago in 1928.) Rapp, Rapp & Hendrickson had closed its Santa Fe office in 1921 after the deaths of two of the partners, while another early Santa Fe–style architect, T. Charles Gaastra, had relocated to the larger city of Albuquerque, leaving the field open to Meem and McCormick. Their first clients were fellow Sunmount patients, but their reputation spread quickly by word of mouth through the city's network of business leaders and well-to-do newcomers.[12]

John Gaw Meem was one of those fortunate people who discover a passion and find a way to make it their life's work. He had the necessary talent, work ethic, and technical skills, of course, along with another requisite—fortuitous timing. Santa Fe—then emerging in the American imagination as an exotic, sun-baked Shangri-La—was the right place; the right time was that two-decade pause between the World Wars—the period when the desire to preserve and build upon America's regional traditions had stirred, but before this inclination had been called into question by Modernism.

A final, intangible factor was Meem's personality, which allowed a rare chemistry to develop with many clients. His charm derived from a modest personality, a mixture of the example of his missionary father and the Latin American milieu of his youth. He was further shaped by the Southern ideal of the chivalrous officer imbued in VMI students, by the example of his uncle's professional demeanor, and, finally, by the relaxed camaraderie of Sunmount and Santa Fe. It wasn't just what was said between Meem and his clients, but also what was not said—the nonverbal give and take of gesture and body language. Remembering John Meem years after his death, his friends attribute the pleasure of his company partly to his inquisitive mind and erudition, but also to his genuine interest in others. He had stimulating things to say, certainly, but he also had an unusual ability to draw people out. Meem knew how to ask questions and then be quiet and listen, how to identify common interests, and how to allow imaginations and enthusiasms to mingle.

Many of Meem's clients were women ten to twenty years older than he was, well-to-do individualists with opinions and accomplishments of their own: Mary Austin, the popular novelist of Indians and the Southwest; Alice Bemis Taylor, who established the Colorado Springs Fine Arts Center; and Ruth Hanna McCormick Simms, a congresswoman from Illinois and later Albuquerque civic activist; also Mrs. Ashley Pond, Mary Vilura Conkey, Amelia Hollenback, Elinor Gregg, and others less well known to the public. Office correspondence documents

Meem during the late 1920s.

show many of these friendships progressed to an affectionate informality. Mamie Meadors, the main contact for three Sunmount veterans who asked Meem to design them a set of cottages, became, through genial repartee, "the principal representative of a powerful syndicate." Eleanor Brownell, headmistress of the Shipley School for girls outside Philadelphia, and her fellow teacher, Alice Howland, for whom Meem designed a summer home and later a retirement house in Santa Fe, evolved from Miss Howland and Miss Brownell to the "Hownells"—this contraction their suggestion to him, a confiding gift of familiarity.[13]

Even the occasional demanding or indecisive client was met with tact and good humor. When construction drawings detailing already approved schematic plans were mailed to one couple, they responded the morning of their arrival with a three-page single-spaced list of changes, followed that evening by another three pages, and over the next two weeks by a steady stream of letters filled with adjustments and self-reversals. As his staff rushed the time-consuming revisions to avoid delaying the waiting building contractor, Meem diplomatically wrote the couple that "[f]or a little while the Firm of Proctor and Proctor had gotten so far ahead of the firm of Meem & McCormick that we felt swamped. Slowly we have emerged and a great help was Mrs. Proctor's final drawing showing all the changes which in a way summarized everything." "Your angelic disposition," acknowledged Dr. Proctor, "has never been more clearly displayed than in the way you have accepted the proposed changes." By the end of the 1920s, Meem had become Santa Fe's architect of choice.[14]

During his first five years of practice, Meem designed an average of four houses and one nonresidential building a year. A major addition to La Fonda in 1927 demonstrated his ability to handle large projects. Meem's winning entry in the 1930 design competition for the Laboratory of Anthropology—funded by John D. Rockefeller Jr.—brought national attention,

Mrs. Emory Steadman, an early client (1926).

opposite
Addition to La Fonda Hotel by Meem (1927). (T. Harmon Parkhurst)

Laboratory of Anthropology (1930).

Carlos Vierra Residence, designed by Vierra (1921). (Wesley Bradfield)

reinforced four years later by the publication of his modernistic, poured concrete Colorado Springs Fine Arts Center. By the time the University of New Mexico (UNM) in Albuquerque named Meem its campus architect in 1933, he was preeminent in the state and the best-known Southwest architect. Throughout the Great Depression, the firm's work was evenly split between residences and public buildings—an average of four each per year.[15]

The first six houses Meem designed in 1925 and early 1926 show a clear debt to his mentor, Carlos Vierra. Vierra's own house, begun in 1918 and largely completed by the time Meem returned from Denver in 1924, epitomized Santa Fe style. In Vierra's hands, the style's trademark flat-roofed, adobe forms took on a rounded, sculptural monumentality. While the house's terraced forms reflect Vierra's emphasis of Pueblo antecedents, the carved porch brackets represent an equal admixture of local Spanish Colonial elements. Glass windows had been almost nonexistent in Pueblo and Spanish times, so the early style adopted wood casement windows from the Craftsman style, and topped them with hewn wooden lintels patterned on historic porch beams. Meem and most others termed this composite the Spanish-Pueblo style.[16]

Although Meem's first few house forms were somewhat stiff and his floor plans occasionally awkward, his work matured rapidly. By early 1926, elements that would recur throughout his later houses first appeared. Before Meem, local designers often terminated porches with thin masonry piers or free-standing posts, which left these *portales* looking like insubstantial add-ons. In his design for the Emory Steadman Residence, Meem thickened a corner pier well beyond what was structurally necessary so the porch would appear solid—as if carved from the mass of the house itself. One plan for the Wyles summer house had a deep porch with a built-in fireplace at one end; this is the first appearance of the living porch that Meem developed into a trademark of his work. This

Emory Steadman Residence (1926).

Meadors-Staples-Anthony Residences (1925).

house also premiered rustic stone retaining walls and foundations, which allowed Meem to step building masses down uneven sites, thereby evoking Anasazi ruins.[17]

For Vierra, as for many of Meem's clients, sun-baked adobe bricks—preferably made on the site in the traditional manner—were essential to authenticity. Meem wrote to the Steadmans that he "had an experienced adobe man look over the site yesterday and he gave us as his opinion that the soil there is much too gravelly to make adobes." Meem advised instead having them made "somewhere else on good adobe ground," which would cost thirty dollars per thousand adobes delivered. (A moderate-sized house uses seven to ten thousand adobes.) However, many clients worried about maintenance, and Meem generally advised that "our experience is that adobe will cost a little less, but that in the long run is not as satisfactory as a more permanent material, such as hollow tile."[18]

Most houses Meem designed over the years were built of these hollow terra-cotta blocks laid carefully to evoke irregular adobe walls, with rounded parapets executed with fired brick and a finish coat of adobe-colored stucco. His standard bid specifications warned contractors that "the chief characteristics of this building are the irregular contours of its wall surfaces and silhouettes. . . . In general, the masonry is to reflect primitive adobe and therefore is to be laid more by eye than by plumb, square and level." Meem rarely detailed these undulating surfaces and parapets, but instead visited construction sites regularly and preferred contractors who had learned to achieve his desired effect.[19]

SOUTHEAST · ELEVATION ·

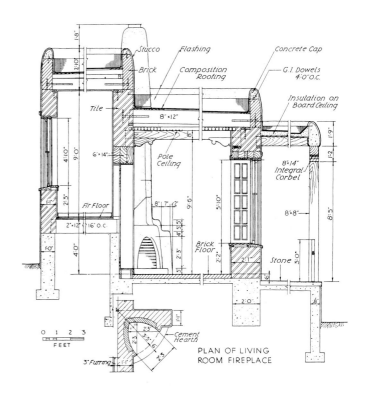

Tom R. Wyles Residence (1926).

Construction cross-section, Mary V. Conkey Residence (1928).

(*American Architect*)

SYNTHESIZING VERNACULAR, BEAUX-ARTS, AND ROMANTIC TRADITIONS

The majority of Santa Fe–style houses in the teens employed the compact, nationally popular bungalow floor plan. A few, such as Carlos Vierra's house, utilized a setback second story in imitation of terraced Indian pueblos, but only rarely did anyone adopt the rectangular courtyard form of the Spanish-Mexican tradition. A certain awkwardness in Meem's first few houses derived largely from his reliance on overly compact plans. But as his detailing matured, he also began to open his house plans out into informal, sprawling compositions now considered hallmarks of Santa Fe style. By mid-1928, Meem had begun to synthesize passages of Beaux-Arts formality, elements from Pueblo and Spanish vernacular traditions, picturesque design strategies, and the demands of his clients' new, informal lifestyles into a personal design mode.

When John Meem entered the field in the 1920s, classicism and the French Beaux-Arts approach to design dominated architectural education and journals. A textbook issued by the Beaux-Arts Institute in New York—*The Study of Architectural Design* by John Harbeson— focused largely on monumental civic buildings and Colonial Revival mansions. Their symmetrical plans and classical details were immediately intelligible to the public as signs of order and clarity. Ample entry halls with grand stairways made the simple action of entering a building into a ritual of civic participation and social hierarchy. Occasionally, Harbeson admitted, a project with unequal components, an irregularly shaped building site, or uneven topography prevented overall symmetry. "Of course," he assured young students, "in any such 'unsymmetrical plan,' there are many features and groups of features that are symmetrical about minor axes." In retrospect, it seems fortuitous that Meem completed only a third of the Beaux-Arts Institute's program. He was introduced to the notion of working from historical precedents and the handling of proportions and details, but not to the often obsessive quest to resolve each design into a completely symmetrical plan instilled in the later years of the program. While Meem would frequently develop secondary symmetrical axes—especially to impart formality to entry sequences or focus attention on a landscape view—the overall asymmetry of most of his building plans and facade compositions was closer to the picturesque adobe buildings of New Mexico.[20]

As Meem's practice expanded in 1927, he recruited Gordon Street from the office of Denver architect Temple Buell. Street had majored in architecture at the University of Kansas and, after serving in World War I, even studied for a time at the Ecole des Beaux-Arts in Paris. He was admired for his beautiful drawing hand and, as Meem's chief draftsman and delineator for five years, strongly represented the Beaux-Arts approach in the office.

An architectural education of this era ideally concluded with a grand tour of Europe. By studying and sketching for a year or two, a student might absorb the proportions and details of one or two architectural periods and thereby become expert in those period revival styles. By the 1920s, architects had also turned their attention to architectural traditions at home, and developed American Colonial and Spanish Revival styles appropriate to particular regions. In lieu of a European tour, Meem immersed himself in the study of historic New Mexican architecture.

During Meem's time at Sunmount Sanitarium, Dr. Mera organized group outings to Hispanic villages and Pueblo Indian dances. When Meem visited the classic Spanish Colonial church at Las Trampas during Lent in 1921, one of his traveling companions was Anne Evans, daughter of a former Colorado governor, who would soon organize the Society for the Preservation and Restoration of New Mexico Mission Churches. By the fall of 1924, Meem was at Acoma Pueblo as the society's supervising architect, making plans for the renovation of its great mission church. Through his supervision of six restorations over the next eight years Meem's knowledge of Spanish Colonial architecture deepened. When residential clients collected historic wood details for their houses, or purchased existing adobe houses to serve as the cores for their new homes, Meem had further opportunities for study.[21]

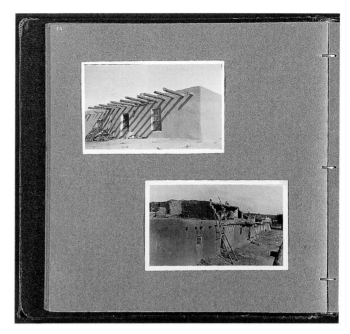

Page from one of Carlos Vierra's six photographic albums on New Mexican architecture.

Carlos Vierra had assembled six photo albums of historic New Mexico architecture, emphasizing Pueblo villages and missions. These went on extended loan to Meem, and ultimately became a permanent part of his office library. Indeed, in 1931, Vierra advised Meem on questions of authenticity for the design of a summer house for Cyrus McCormick Jr. The following year, Vierra, Meem, and McCormick contracted with Lippincott, a leading publisher of architectural monographs, to produce a volume on New Mexico. Meem was to lead in its preparation but, with the demands of his booming practice and the death of Vierra in 1937, the book never materialized. As the Southwestern director for the Historic American Building Survey from its inception in 1935, Meem selected monuments of state architecture to be documented in measured drawings by architects and draftsmen left unemployed by the Great Depression. Three volumes of these drawings became another touchstone of his library.[22]

While Meem's immersion in the regional tradition was consistent with the Beaux-Arts approach to history, he discovered more irregularity than classical symmetry in the local vernacular. Similarly, the early Spanish-Pueblo Revival drew more inspiration from the Romantic movement than the classical tradition. Originating in late eighteenth-century England, Romanticism was popularized in the United States beginning in the 1850s through the works of English theorist John Ruskin and the American house pattern books of Andrew Jackson Downing. (Meem's library included both Ruskin's *Seven Lamps of Architecture* and Downing's *The Architecture of Country Houses*.) In place of the timeless universals of symmetry and proportion found in nature and echoed in classical architecture, Romantics emphasized an individual's subjective, aesthetic experience. One still might experience *beauty* in classical symmetry and proportion, but equally important were experiences of the *sublime* to be found in

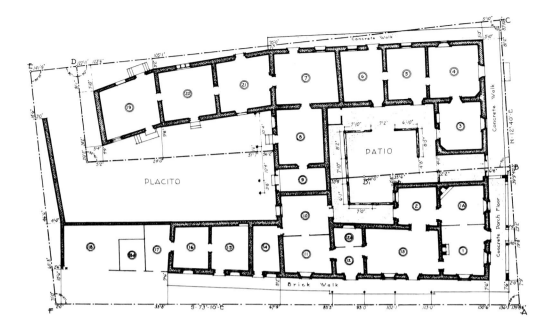

PLACITO

PATIO

Floor plan of Garcia House (about 1800). (Historic American Building Survey, 1940)

vastness and grandeur, and of the *picturesque* found in irregularity and contrast, novelty, and the exotic.[23]

According to the Romantics, a jagged mountain range or immense chasm—either in nature or in a landscape painting—might inspire awe and reverence. But only the occasional monumental building—the soaring interior of a great cathedral, for instance—could evoke comparable sentiments. On a commanding site, a building's windows and porches carefully framing landscape vistas, rather than the building itself, provided the experience of the sublime. This desire to orient windows and porches to the best views, in turn, favored asymmetrical floor plans tailored to the specific character of the site.

The Romantic yearning for connection to nature led to the design of buildings that nestled into the landscape and to the use of local, rustic materials. Meem, for instance, discerned picturesque qualities in the hand-plastered and rain-eroded forms of local adobe buildings. "The result of these two processes," he wrote, "was that all surfaces and outlines adjusted themselves naturally to the requirements of drainage and erosion, thus producing an informal quality which, together with the massiveness of the forms, made them seem utterly appropriate to their setting of eroded flat-topped mesas and plateaus." While the nineteenth-century Romantics favored the imagery of Gothic cathedrals and half-timbered cottages, Spanish missions and terraced Pueblo villages provided an exotic presence in the American Southwest by the 1920s.[24]

Designers in the Romantic tradition also deployed their masses asymmetrically to create picturesque compositions. In the hands of the best designers, this approach also evoked the incremental construction of vernacular buildings over time. Picturesque compositions (whether the result of vernacular accretion or a modern architect's creativity) give aesthetic pleasure through what was termed occult symmetry—not one-for-one, bilateral symmetry, but a careful overall balance of mass and detail. In a picturesquely composed building, the eye of the viewer is drawn first to a tower or primary mass positioned a bit off center, then to a secondary element on the opposite side, back to a lesser element beyond the tower, and so forth over subtly interrelated masses, roofs, dormers, and ornamental accents. In Spanish mission complexes, Meem discerned "an unconscious avoidance of bi-lateral symmetry, but never at the expense of balance," while the large church naves "established the main mass against which were grouped the lesser buildings of the monastery."[25]

Although picturesque composition developed as a pictorial device that freed buildings from classical symmetry, it also had the fortuitous side effect of permitting more flexible floor plans—the better to accommodate various functions and room shapes. Entry halls, living rooms, and dining rooms flowed informally one into another, while the proliferation of porches and terraces mediated the transition between the interior and nature. Meem's youth in Brazil and study of New Mexican architecture gave him a particular understanding of the potentials of porches and open-air courtyards.

The Romantic undercurrent in American architecture surfaced in the work of such leading figures as Henry Hobson Richardson and Frank Lloyd Wright, and in popular Queen Anne–style houses, resort hotels, and rustic country houses. The picturesque approach also burst forth in the regional revivals of the 1920s, most strongly—and most importantly for Meem—in the Spanish Revival. Architects such as George Washington Smith and Wallace Neff of California, Ayres & Ayres of Texas, and Addison Mizner of Florida drew inspiration not only from the Spanish Colonial buildings of their own locales, but also from Mexico, Spain, and the Mediterranean world. Their designs emphasized asymmetric, stuccoed masses with tile roofs and carved stone details on porches, balconies, doors, and windows.[26]

Spanish Revival architects also adapted the traditional courtyard house plan to define sheltered patios and terraces for the increasingly informal outdoor lifestyle of the 1920s. But when they also stretched their house plans to capture views and to accommodate the needs of modern households, they often dispensed with the traditional rectangular courtyard in favor of more informal, sprawling L-, U-, and Y-shaped plans. By keeping their buildings close to the ground, noted one critic, they might "appear . . . as part of the landscape." This informality also favored picturesque composition and evocative, theatrical effects.[27]

Meem was first exposed to this movement in the Denver offices of Fisher & Fisher, who occasionally designed Spanish-style patio houses. After Meem opened his own office, his library included all the key sources on Spanish and Mexican architecture and on the Spanish Revival in America. In his 1927 survey, *The Spanish Home for America*, Rexford Newcomb treated developments in Santa Fe as a unique, half-Spanish, half-Pueblo idiom within this broader movement. Newcomb illustrated Carlos Vierra's house in *The Spanish House* and included Meem's work in his subsequent publications.[28]

By 1928, Meem was drawing from a wide range of inspirations: classical formality and Beaux-Arts design; his own close study of local Pueblo and Spanish-Colonial buildings; the example of the Spanish Revival, especially in southern California; picturesque composition techniques; and the abundant opportunities in New Mexico for landscape views and solar orientation. The house in which Meem first reconciled these ideas and sources—one of his finest designs—was the Mary Vilura Conkey Residence of 1928 (see illustrations on pp. 135–139). Over the next five years, in a series of major Spanish-Pueblo Revival houses, Meem seamlessly blended these components in ever varying proportions.[29]

Every house design began with the collection of background information. A jotted list of required rooms from a client conference, such as the one quoted earlier for the Ferdinand Koch Residence, along with a notation of the client's style preference—in the early years it was almost always "The Spanish Pueblo style" or "in the native style"—sufficed for modest projects. Even for the largest, most lavish country houses, the program could be summarized in no more than three single-spaced typed pages. Some clients had collected historic wooden ceilings, porches, and doors; others sought Meem's advice about obtaining similar architectural antiques for inclusion in their houses. Lists of available details with measurements and sketches were assembled before design commenced.

"I really would like to see the various sites because these always suggest ideas in connection with the plans," Meem wrote one new client in Albuquerque. There, on the level flood plain of the Rio Grande, he usually found a small rise or mound to give the house prominence and lift it a few feet for better views. On the rugged foothills so favored by his Santa Fe clients, the first consideration was often the identification of a relatively level spot, large enough for the house and surrounding patios, which could be economically developed without expensive foundation and retaining walls or a long access road. Many clients inclined toward the highest spot on their property, but Meem typically coaxed them off the ridge tops to more practical sites. Solar orientation remained a secondary siting consideration until the second half of the 1930s, when Meem more fully developed his idea of a portal deep enough to serve as a living room with one side open to views and solar gain.[30]

The single most important factor influencing building site selection, however, was the strong desire of all Meem's clients for grand landscape views. This was a fairly straightforward consideration in Albuquerque, where the Sandia Mountains dominated to the east, and in Colorado

Springs where Pikes Peak to the southwest was the obvious focus. But with the Sangre de Cristos and Sunmount Hill immediately to the east of Santa Fe, the Cerillos Hills and the Ortiz, San Pedro, and Sandia Mountains to the southwest, the Jemez to the west, and the Española Valley and Pajarito Plateau to the northwest, house sites there often provided two or more stunning views. A concentration of Meem houses within a four-block radius of Sunmount Sanitorium, for instance, took advantage of views of Sunmount Hill, the Sandias, and the Jemez. Site sketches made in the field as well as floor plan studies done in the office note the directions of views as well as the north arrow. Everyone understood that the best views would go to the public entertaining areas, primarily the living room and its adjoining porch or terrace, then to the master bedroom, and possibly to the dining room, a breakfast room, or guest suite.

As Meem began to develop a floor plan back in his office, the Beaux-Arts emphasis on building type conventions came into play. His sense of the appropriate sizes for different rooms and how they should be grouped and connected to each other reflected his understanding of the patterns of social decorum. This understanding derived both from his architectural education,

Mary V. Conkey Residence, view from the southwest (1928). (Ansel Adams)

J. R. Cole Residence (1949). View to the southwest of Cerrillos Hills, San Pedro and Sandia Mountains. (Laura Gilpin)

opposite
Location of Sunmount Sanitarium and major Meem houses in southeastern Santa Fe indicating primary landscape views. (George C. Pearl)

Site sketch of the second Eleanor Brownell and Alice Howland Residence. It identifies landscape views and roughs out the living room, bedroom, and service wings. (1941).

best summarized in room adjacency diagrams of the period, but also from his own social experiences in the expatriate art colony. Rooms were organized in three primary groupings: the middle public entrance with living and dining rooms, the private, family bedrooms on one side, and the kitchen, pantry, and maid's room to the other. This general pattern is still evident in many houses today. (The post—World War II ranch house plan, for instance, places the public entry at the living room which flows into the dining room; to one side are the private bedrooms and bath; to the other are the garage with a second, informal entrance for groceries on their way to the kitchen.)

In Meem's more elaborate houses, the public realm typically included a formal entry hall, a living room with attached outdoor living area, a dining room, sometimes a library, and the occasional ballroom. A hallway typically led from the living room to the family bedrooms, each with a private bath, and, sometimes, also a sleeping porch or private terrace. A butler's serving pantry provided a noise buffer between the dining room and kitchen, which led to a storage pantry; a cellar with furnace, laundry, and storage; a garage; and the servants' quarters with a bathroom and, often, a sitting porch. Typically there was only one connection each between the public and private sections, and the public and service groupings. The lack of a direct con-

nection between the bedrooms and service areas distanced the family from servants. In more modest, middle-class houses, the entry opened directly into the living room, which provided circulation between the other rooms. The service core shrank to a kitchen with extensive cabinets in place of a pantry and with many new laborsaving appliances that compensated the housewives for the absence of live-in servants. Such spatial hierarchies are so conventional and taken for granted that the layperson only becomes aware of them if they are violated—for example, if a bathroom opens directly off a living room. However, an architect must be conscious of these relations to avoid violating them and to develop plans that bring adjacent functions as closely together as possible to avoid wasted hallway space.

Meem usually began his floor plans by locating the formal entry and living room because they mediated between the other two groupings, and they would command the best views, while also providing the largest mass for the exterior composition. Next came other rooms that were to have views, primarily the dining room and master bedroom. Bedroom wings were located with an eye to providing privacy, while service functions were placed out of view of the formal entrance. As Meem began to fine-tune the size and relationships of the rooms, he checked to see that every room had windows on two walls, and, where possible, on three or even

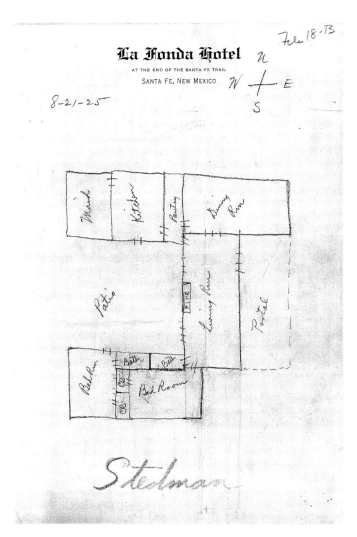

La Fonda Hotel

AT THE END OF THE SANTA FE TRAIL

SANTA FE, NEW MEXICO

Feb 18·73

8-21-25

Steadman

Sketch plan of Steadman Residence on La Fonda Hotel stationery (August 21, 1925).

four sides of major rooms. In this era before air conditioning, this ensured cross ventilation, as well as natural light and views.

Meem occasionally roughed out a floor plan in the first client conference, but only if the requirements were simple, and he was already familiar with the site or others like it on the hills above Santa Fe. Unmoved by the Modernist desire for entirely novel solutions, he operated on the assumption that design conventions and his growing expertise would provide the proper starting point for a design. Each house would assume its proper individuality as a result of the specifics of its site and the personalities and needs of the client. In an entirely new setting, and for more ambitious programs, Meem developed as many as fifteen interim designs before reaching an optimal plan.

If exterior composition typically remained in the back of Meem's mind in these early phases, it became central as the plan neared resolution. Exterior wall elevation drawings and, occasionally, clay models aided in the study of exterior compositions, which were usually picturesque rather than classical and rigidly symmetrical. Meem positioned the living room mass, or a partial second story (if there was to be one) off center to provide the focal point of the composition. Against this he balanced a secondary mass— a master bedroom, for instance, with a portal stretching between these masses. But the best picturesque designs unfold as a set of asymmetrical, yet balanced, compositions as one moves around the building. Like many other picturesque house designers, Meem concentrated on the composition of the facade visible from the public approach, and then on facades facing terraces and gardens. While many picturesque revival styles employed a mixture of textured materials for additional variety, Meem's emphasis of flat-roofed forms and adobe surfaces unified his compositions and related them to the dry, brown landscape. "The building is designed to fit the contours," he wrote to one client, and to another he noted he was "terracing the house down to fit the contours."[31]

Preliminary design took from one day to a few weeks. At this point, a preliminary floor plan, sometimes with an alternate, and a facade or perspective drawing went to the client for comment. Their responses typically required at least a few changes, and, after fine-tuning, the preparation of detailed construction drawings began. Ranging from five to twenty sheets, these working drawings typically took about six weeks to complete. The attention lavished on the drawing and lettering of architectural plans during this era became a further demonstration of the craftsmanship of the architect and his staff and an indication of the quality of execution expected from the builder.

In eclectic revival houses, the architect's pleasing exterior composition, elegant entry sequence, sure handling of proportion, and historically correct details demonstrated his taste, and by implication the taste and social standing of his clients, some of whom actively participated in their house designs. The picturesque names of large estates were often selected at this stage so they could be included on the working drawings. In the East, country house names such as the Biltmore, Blairsdale, Maxwell Court, Timberline, and The Moorings evoked images of castles and English country houses, while, in California, Hacienda del Pozo de Verona, Dias Felices, and Casa del Herrero recalled Mediterranean villas. Meem's great houses included La Resolana (the sunny gathering place on the south side of a building), Las Acequias (for the historic irrigation ditches on a large estate), Las Dos Hermanas (the two sisters), Los Piñones (the piñon pines), Los Poblanos (the cluster of ranches), and La Quinta (the estate).[32]

Although Meem typically adapted traditional Spanish and Pueblo floor plan types freely to meet contemporary living patterns, he occasionally designed full courtyard houses. The climate at 5,000 ft (1740 m) in Albuquerque where Los Poblanos was built in 1932 is moderate enough for its courtyard to provide the primary circulation. But at 7,200 ft (2195 m) in the hills above Santa Fe, where the first Brownell-Howland house went up in 1930, the weather was harsh enough for the clients to ask Meem to design glass inserts to transform its portales into enclosed corridors around the courtyard.

Like his southern California contemporaries, Meem more frequently opened the Hispanic courtyard prototype out into more informal shapes, which he referred to in correspondence variously as "an 'L' shaped building," "a 'U' shaped house," or "our 'H' type plan." The development of narrow, radiating arms facilitated cross ventilation, light, and views; permitted the separation of the bedroom, public, and service room groupings into distinct wings; helped define exterior terraces; and enhanced the possibilities for picturesque composition. Such plans increased exterior wall surfaces and, as a result, construction costs, which became prohibitive for some clients. Meem developed an alternate scheme to cut costs for one client but advised her that, "to do so, however, you will notice that it is a pretty compact mass and we have lost the picturesqueness of the patio."[33]

COUNTRY RESIDENCES

"My wife and I have decided to build a little vacation establishment near Santa Fe," wrote Cyrus McCormick Jr. to his acquaintance John D. Rockefeller Jr. in early 1930. "We chose John Meem as our architect," who "has by far the best architectural office in New Mexico" and "is able to bring to his problems a greater artistic tradition." Then in the planning stages, the McCormick estate in Nambe 16 miles (26 km) north of Santa Fe may well have seemed a "little vacation establishment" to both the son of the inventor of the mechanized reaper and the son of the head of Standard Oil (who was then the wealthiest man in the world), for both belonged to the business oligarchy that emerged in late nineteenth-century America as a result of industrialization. The McCormick Residence and a handful of other country residences allowed Meem to refine his approach to residential design and helped set the tone for year-round, more modest houses.[34]

Concentrated around financial centers in the northeast, Chicago, and St. Louis, these families of the *Social Register* fostered elite universities, private schools, and country clubs, as well as suburban enclaves, summer resorts, and country estates. Many families circulated annually among several houses. The wealthiest purchased large tracts of farm and forest, where they built grand, historical revival houses, often incorporating architectural fragments collected while traveling in Europe.[35]

This business elite discovered New Mexico early in the twentieth century, but even after the construction of a few summer residences, the state remained an exotic outpost. Absorption with native architecture and arts substituted for European and American Colonial antiquity, while sightseeing, horseback riding, and fly-fishing replaced golf or tennis at the local country club. Families with children often summered at large resorts such as Newport, Rhode Island, and Lake Geneva, Wisconsin, where they might meet potential marriage partners. As a result, New Mexico at first attracted unmarried women and older couples. This began to change in the late 1920s with the establishment of private schools: the Los Alamos Ranch School, Fountain Valley School in Colorado Springs, and the Sandia School for Girls in Albuquerque—Meem was the architect for each school.[36]

Cyrus McCormick Jr., as much as any of Meem's clients, desired authenticity for his estate. The one hundred acres he assembled from sixteen property owners consisted of historic long lot field allotments on either side of the Rio Nambe. Along with irrigation ditches and existing houses, this property formed an authentic Spanish Colonial agricultural landscape. With the advice of Carlos Vierra, who collaborated on this project, McCormick collected forty-six historic architectural fragments for reuse in his house. These doors, corbel brackets, and entire ceilings all dated to the Spanish and Mexican eras and, save for one whitewashed ceiling, excluded mid-nineteenth-century American Territorial period detailing. When the time came to construct nine corner fireplaces and plaster the walls of the main house, experienced women were hired from nearby Nambe Pueblo. McCormick's desire to stick "strictly to the spirit of the architecture and the method of living in this country" even meant that the main house was to be illuminated solely by candles and lamps.[37]

Meem converted two existing adobe farmhouses into guest cottages and designed a new caretaker's house, a four-car garage with attached quarters for the chauffeur's family, a stable for eight riding and four farm horses, a cottage for ranch hands, and a shed to accommodate a one-year supply of firewood. Repeated trips to the site, seventeen study plans, and a clay model sculpted by Vierra contributed to Meem's design for the main house.

One elevated, but arid, site with fine views was rejected in favor of a knoll surrounded by mature trees at the edge of the old fields. Nevertheless, an auto court formed by the house and guest quarters, the entry courtyard, a rooftop terrace, and the McCormicks' bedroom each commanded views of the Sangre

Model of Cyrus McCormick Jr. Residence, Las Acequias Ranch, Nambe, 1930 plan. Built in 1931 with later revisions. (George C. Pearl)

McCormick Residence, by Carlos Vierra (1930), as seen from the southwest.

Amelia Hollenbeck Residence from the southwest (1932). (Ansel Adams)

de Cristo Mountains to the east. A final shuttered view of the mountains draws visitors along the main portal toward the bedroom wing. In a sense, Meem's plan also creates separate modules for the master bedroom suite, a studio, the study and living room, the kitchen and dining room, and the servants' quarters. Since this was designed as a summer house, these modules are linked by covered breezeways (see illustrations on pp. 78–85).[38]

Amelia Hollenback of Brooklyn, New York, who also had a summer home in the Poconos, purchased a hillside near Sunmount. She assembled a set of antique architectural details that equaled the McCormicks' collection. Her corbels, *vigas* (log beams), doors, and ceilings came from the seventeenth-century missions at Gran Quivera and Acoma, from the Tesuque and San Ildefonso pueblos, and from the Spanish-Mexican villages of Peralta, Bernalillo, Las Trampas, and San Miguel del Vado (see illustrations on pp. 73, 104–105, 110–111).

Meem unfolded the linear plan for the Hollenback house along a contour of the steep hillside site. This gave the master bedroom, living room, portal, and terrace all a panoramic view of the Jemez Mountains. Hollenback had a particular affinity for Pueblo villages and hoped the house would "settle comfortably and graciously on the hillside." Meem obliged her with terraced masses that nestle into the hillside (see illustrations on pp. 70–72). Seen from the main approach—a view photographed by Ansel Adams soon after its completion—Meem's picturesque composition is crowned by a second-story guest suite, from which the eye moves down to the projecting living room, then left to the bedroom wing, back right to the service wing as it steps down to the garages, and, finally, to the textured stone foundations and retaining walls that reach out into the landscape.[39]

The Chase Residence, designed in 1930, also combined two-story, terraced Pueblo forms with Spanish Colonial–style wooden details. There, Meem clustered the servant quarters and work areas around a service courtyard, while projecting a guest wing and living room west and north to the edge of the hilltop site to claim the view over the Española Valley to the upper Jemez Mountains. Lifted to the second floor, the family bedrooms, a studio and rooftop terrace commanded this view even more.

Frank D. Chase headed an architectural and engineering firm of his own in Chicago and had received some attention from national architectural journals for his Milwaukee Journal Building and Campana Factory Building in Batavia, Illinois. Unlike Hollenback and the McCormicks, who insisted on authentic adobe construction, Chase wanted his house to "be as near fireproof as possible," which meant reinforced concrete, hollow clay tile, and adobe-colored cement stucco. Sensing an opportunity to advance his professional reputation, and wanting to please a fellow architect, Meem and his staff lavished as much attention on this project as on the larger McCormick commission. They produced at least fifteen preliminary floor plans, studied the smallest details with great care, and created a superb aerial perspective representing the house's composition and magnificent view. "Frankly," wrote Meem to Chase, "I believe it will be about the nicest building turned out of our office, if it goes through."[40]

The Chases had initiated the project during a summer visit to Santa Fe in 1929, emboldened by their paper profits in the Wall Street bull market. But after the market crashed that September, Chase crisscrossed the Midwest and eastern seaboard searching for work, writing periodically to Meem on railroad and hotel stationery. In October 1930, he admitted, "[b]usiness is so poor and the prospects so discouraging for the immediate future that I have decided not to build next spring. I therefore wish that you would stop work on the plans." But within a month, he instructed Meem to "complete the plans at once. I'm satisfied that the entire country is realizing

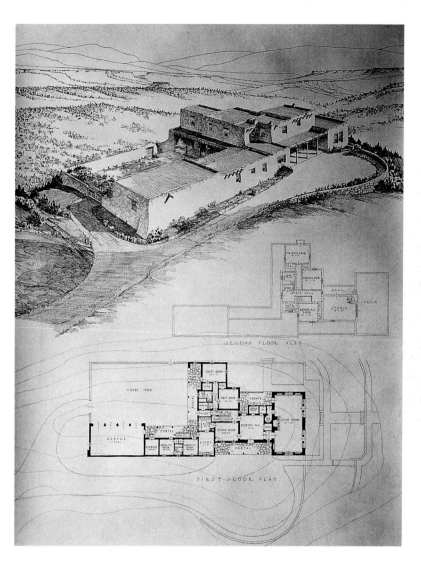

"Residence for Mr. and Mrs. Frank D. Chase" (1930). (Gordon Street)

that we have turned the corner, and that conditions are improving. . . . [I want] to take advantage of present low prices (and I do not think they will remain at present levels very long). So please rush the work . . . ." By January, he was confident that "we turned the corner with the first of the year. . . . In 90 days there will [be] a marked improvement . . . however my last wire was intended merely to tell you not to work overtime. . . ."[41]

But by this point Meem had already paid over $1,000 in staff wages out of his own pocket for the Chase Residence. Allowing a comparable amount for office overhead and his own time, the equivalent of perhaps $40,000 today had already gone into the design. When Meem finally sent a token first billing in September 1931, Chase responded, "I have been circulating down East on and off for the last six weeks trying to line up some business and have been successful in getting a small number of small jobs. . . . It seems absurd to tell you that I can not spare $200.00, but such is the case. I have been extremely hard up for a long time." Whatever Meem might have thought to himself about such a setback at the height of the Great Depression— whatever those of us possessing less Christian charity might be inclined to say in such a situation—Meem responded the day after receiving Chase's letter: "Please don't let the statement we sent you be on your mind at all. Whenever things pick up with you it will be time enough . . . . I am sure it is very largely a matter of luck and that our turn to draw up the belt will come sooner or later."[42]

The project had long since been written off the office books when a check for two hundred dollars and this note arrived from Chase: "It's difficult to realize that its nearly 7 years since I've seen you—seven long hard years—at least some of them were. We are busy again. . . . I congratulate you on the Fine Arts Center at Colorado Springs. It's splendid and both Mrs. Chase and I have studied it with pleasure, and now and then we study our home." Meem replied with characteristic grace, that he "did not know when I have received a more pleasant surprise," and "If you decide eventually to build a house, I assure you that it is going to give me great pleasure to work on it with you." The Chase Residence would be the most significant house designed by Meem to go unbuilt.[43]

If lavish country houses permitted the fullest play of romantic, regionalist sensibilities, Meem's designs for middle-income families represent a distillation of his approach to essentials. His most common design solution was his H-shaped plan, which situated the living room crosswise at the middle of the design with a deeper bedroom wing on one side, and the dining room, kitchen, and garage on the other. This permitted an entry portal in one crook of the H and a sheltered, private patio in the other. In lieu of antique architectural details, a few carved brackets on the portal, a folk Territorial entry door, colorful tile accents, and a corner fireplace with a painted surround imparted regional character. Often constrained by small city lots that lacked a landscape vista, the location of the street became the key siting consideration, with the entrance made clearly visible and bedrooms positioned for privacy.

Although John Gaw Meem matured as an architect just as the Great Depression struck, those long, hard years would never cause him to draw up his belt. In fact, the peak of his creativity from the Conkey Residence in 1928 to the outbreak of World War II at the end of 1941 saw a constant flow of commissions, first from private patrons and then, after 1934, New Deal–funded public buildings, which allowed him to put his stamp on the civic identity of the region. Various factors coalesced in Meem's design idiom. He and his clients shared a belief in the desirability of continuing the region's historical traditions. Low labor costs permitted extensive use of handcrafted details, while Meem identified and cultivated building contractors who could simulate the appearance of adobe in modern materials. In his own firm, his efficient office manager, Ruth Heflin; the talented designer and delineator, Gordon Street; and a succession of younger architects carried much of the day-to-day burden. Through most of the 1930s, Meem even finessed the increasingly strident Modernist attack on the sort of regional historicism that was the very basis of his creativity.

RECONCILING TRADITION AND MODERNITY

Meem's growing reputation brought an invitation to speak at the American Institute of Architects' annual convention at San Antonio in 1931. In this, his first statement of principles, Meem emphasized the inherent connection of rounded, weathered adobe forms to the land and the inspiration for picturesque compositions found in terraced pueblos and Spanish missions. (Although the possibilities for landscape views figure frequently in client correspondence and conference notes, Meem curiously never mentions this factor in this talk or in subsequent articles.) He concluded his talk:

> This is the machine age and the buildings are typified by machine precision, by the use of steel and glass. But our little city had no industries and it does not produce machines. Our problem is not how to get maximum light but how to keep out the glare of abundant sunlight. The thick walls and cool shadows of the traditional form solve this admirably. Every modern demand can be met within the traditional forms and still be true to the demands of function and expression of simple materials. We are trying not to imitate the spirit of the times in the great city but to be true to the spirit of the times in our own section, thus preserving still vital ancient values and adding to the joy and charm of living.

Although Meem sounds the Modernist buzzwords—machine age, precision, demands of function, expression of materials—he also insists that this modern age is not a single monolithic condition dictating a single solution but varies from place to place, dictating regional variation.[44]

Commissioned early the following year to design the Colorado Springs Fine Arts Center, Meem wrote to Betty Hare, the pivotal member of the building committee, "I of course am thrilled at the opportunity of designing a building strictly in keeping with modern times." In addition to providing for a community theater, Meem would have to balance the Modernist tendencies of a progressive art school with the regional aspirations of a museum of Southwestern art. In fact, this made Meem "feel more confident in tackling this problem because its modernity will in a sense be based on a tradition I understand. I have the feeling that to simply express the function of the materials in a building without reference to past experience leaves the design a little empty, a little less rich than it otherwise might be."[45]

Just as work on the design of the center was commencing, a young graduate of the Cambridge School of Architecture and Landscape Architecture (a women's affiliate of MIT) named Faith Bemis entered Meem's office. The niece of Meem's leading patron in Colorado Springs, Alice Bemis Taylor, Bemis brought a more immediate exposure to emerging Modernist currents and such books as Sheldon Cheney's *New World Architecture* with her into the office. She had acquired her interest in architecture from her father, Albert Farwell Bemis, who wanted to be an architect himself but was persuaded by his father to manage the family manufacturing company. Albert Bemis retired early from business to devote himself to research on prefabricated housing at MIT, where he coauthored a groundbreaking study on the subject in 1933. That summer of 1933, Meem, then thirty-eight, married Faith Bemis, thirty-one. Not that any traditionalist architect in those years could avoid the challenge of Modernism, but when Meem opened a Christmas present to find an English polemic entitled *The Modern House* inscribed "Best Wishes for a Very Merry Christmas 1934/John from Father B," the dilemma of tradition versus Modernism came closer to home than for most.[46]

John and Faith Bemis Meem on their wedding day (1933).

With the Fine Arts Center under construction, Meem wondered in a 1934 *American Architect* article, "Given this rich heritage of traditional [Southwestern] form, what should be the architect's approach to modern design problems in this particular region? . . . The answer," he replied, reasonably enough, "partly depends on what one's concept of the 'modern' movement in architecture is." Most proponents of Modernism held that architecture should express the spirit of the scientific, machine age through the forthright use of such industrial materials as steel, concrete, and plate glass, and also express a building's structure and functions. Standardization, precision, and efficiency—not the recreation of historic styles and ornament—were the honest signs of this scientific age.[47]

Meem recalled that his own thinking was clarified by a talk at the 1931 AIA conference by the great Finnish-American architect Eliel Saarinen. "He felt that great epochs in architecture were developed by an intuitive feeling for what he called, 'the fundamental form of the time.' This form is a composite of everything in a people's culture, in their way of thinking and living." Rather than fetishizing industrial materials, Meem embraced this need to intuitively reconcile peoples' traditions with modern technology and contemporary social patterns. To Meem's way of thinking, terraced Indian pueblos were substantial aboriginal structures of "utmost directness and simplicity," and "the earliest expression of an American Fundamental Form." Out of necessity and intuition, Spanish Colonists and early American settlers adhered to these "essential characteristics . . . flat topped rectangular masses devoid of ornament, the aesthetic effect depending almost entirely on the relative proportions of the masses." "Particularly in the Southwest," Meem concluded, "architects who use old forms need do no violence to the ideals of contemporary architectural thoughts. On the contrary, the fundamental form of the time can best be expressed in a language native to the region. These ancient shapes are modern!"[48]

Meem's monumental, sculptural adobe forms echoed the massive, flat-roofed Art Deco buildings of the era and also paralleled the growing influence of Cubist abstraction in the work of the Taos and Santa Fe art colonies. A first wave of artists in the teens and twenties had painted the tower facade of the church at Ranchos de Taos, typically augmented by a picturesque procession or dance. But around 1930, a younger generation—from photographers Paul Strand and Laura Gilpin to painters John Marin and Georgia O'Keeffe—turned their attention to the massive, undulating buttresses at the rear of the church and dispensed with the inclusion of any people who might distract from their asymmetrical, abstract compositions. In formal, aesthetic terms, Meem's building designs were entirely in keeping with this Modernist-influenced generation of visual artists.[49]

Meem with model of Colorado Springs Fine Arts Center (1934). (Tyler Dingee about 1950)

Colorado Springs Fine Arts Center (1934). (Ernest Knee)

Meem's most convincing demonstration of this philosophy is the Colorado Springs Fine Arts Center. His design is enriched by a double coded symbolism rarely seen in those years. The building was undeniably modern in its exposed concrete construction. But the careful craftsmanship that went into the construction of the concrete form work remained apparent in wood grain patterns left in those concrete surfaces. Likewise, sand and gravel aggregates were carefully selected to give the concrete not a gray but a light beige tone, which reinforced the Pueblo evocation of the center's terraced massing.[50]

The daring Modern Regionalism of the Fine Arts Center won Meem national and international recognition but did not lead to a new idiom in his work. The strong historicist inclinations of his clients back in New Mexico, and of Meem himself, meant that his subsequent work would continue to be in "the old Santa Fe or Pueblo Spanish style." However, Meem's conviction that his work was thoroughly modern, while also rooted in a valued regional tradition, imbued his subsequent designs with a sureness of proportion and a monumental dignity akin to the Fine Arts Center. The precision and latent classicism of the Fine Arts Center, nevertheless, contributed to the definition of Meem's second historicist idiom—the Territorial Revival.

Zimmerman Library, University of New Mexico, Albuquerque (1936). (Laura Gilpin)

Los Poblanos Ranch, Albuquerque (1932). (Laura Gilpin)

Tilney Residence (1929). (Ansel Adams)

opposite

Robert Tilney Residence with the foothills of the Sangre de Cristos
in the background (1929). (T. Harmon Parkhurst)

TERRITORIAL REVIVAL

This revival drew elements selectively from the provincial Greek Revival buildings of the American territorial period, particularly those erected between the U.S. occupation of the Southwest in 1846 and the advent of the railroad in 1880. These buildings continued the flat-roofed, adobe vernacular but added whitewashed milled lumber porch posts with molding capitals, triangular window lintels recalling temple pediments, and protective brick cornices evoking classical entablatures.

The first formulation of the Santa Fe style in the teens had included only one Territorial-era detail—brick copings—which Meem employed as early as 1925 in the Ashley Pond Residence. However, his understanding of the origins of this frontier strain of classicism and his name for his new revival style did not crystallize until about 1935. The 1928 Conkey Residence established white pedimented lintels as an appropriate way to detail the doors and windows of otherwise Spanish-Pueblo Revival designs. Other clients such as Mrs. Robert Tilney desired greater formality, for instance, when she requested "nothing heavy or Indian," "as little Mexican as possible," and "interior of house to be American Colonial in spirit." To complement the classical moldings of her American Colonial interior, Meem quoted the regional classicism of the Territorial era for her 1929 house. The many operable shutters reinforced this connection to the eastern Colonial Revival. But apparently Meem thought New Mexico's classicism had come north from Mexico in the 1820s and '30s, rather than west from the States after 1846 (as subsequent scholarship would establish), for he described the exterior of the Tilney Residence as "Mexican Colonial Style" and included a sprinkling of wrought iron and arched openings.[51]

Meem omitted these few Spanish-Mexican accents from the 1931 Isabel Eccles Residence in Santa Fe and Los Poblanos, the 1932 house of Albert and Ruth Simms in Albuquerque (see illustrations on pp. 140–147). Both display the mature revival-style combination of milled porticos, pedimented lin-

tels, and brick copings. But Meem's use of hand-adzed, as well as smooth, milled posts and brown, as well as white, trim contrasts rustic variety with crisp formality. This emerging style also offered the possibility of tailoring architectural images for specific locations and institutions. The 1932 McLane Residence, for instance, employs basic Territorial Revival details, but also includes Carpenter Gothic Revival scrollwork and a bracketed bay window—more emphatic icons of the Anglo-American frontier appropriate for Colorado Springs. (The parallel mid-nineteenth-century fusion in California of Mexican adobe construction and tile roofs with provincial Greek Revival–detailing introduced by Yankee traders was also revived during the late 1920s as the Monterey style.)[52]

Two major commissions in 1934 completed the development of the Territorial Revival: a semi-public community center designed for Ruth and Albert Simms's Los Poblanos Ranch and the Federal Emergency Recovery Act (FERA) Building (now known as the Villagra Building), Santa Fe's first New Deal structure. Ruth Hanna McCormick Simms, the former Congresswoman, had befriended Meem and saw her entertainment building—La Quinta—and a nearby house for her brother-in-law, John Simms, as Meem's chance "to show Albuquerque what you can do in this line" (see illustrations on pp. 74–75, 124–125). For the FERA and Simms projects, Meem purified the style of rustic finishes and Spanish details, instead emphasizing crisp corners, white classical details, and symmetrical compositions. He continued to refer to this

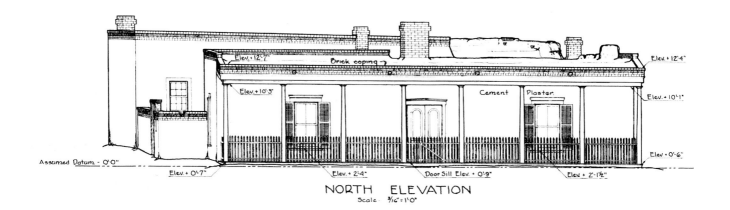

Elev.+12'7"   Brick coping   Elev.+12'4"

Elev.+10'3"   Cement   Plaster   Elev.+10'1"

Elev.+0'6"

Assumed Datum - 0'0"

Elev.+0'7"   Elev.+2'4"   Door Sill Elev.+0'9"   Elev.+2'-1½"

NORTH ELEVATION
Scale ¾₆" = 1'-0"

Borrego House (about 1870). (Historic American Building Survey, 1940)

James McLane Residence, Colorado Springs (1932). (Chris Wilson)

mode as Spanish-Colonial, apparently acknowledging the Spanish contribution of flat-roofed adobe forms, as well as the echo of the American Colonial in New Mexico's provincial classicism. Although the style achieved a degree of popularity for homes in Albuquerque and Santa Fe, its most significant impact came through its selection as the unifying style for the State Capitol complex.[53]

In 1934, just as this style was crystallizing, Meem was named the Southwest director of the Historic American Building Survey (HABS). In 1935, his teams of out-of-work architects and draftsmen documented the Pueblo villages and Spanish missions that had provided the inspiration for the Spanish-Pueblo Revival. By 1936, Meem added Territorial-era structures to his documentation wish list and began to describe them and the new buildings he was designing as the Territorial style. In 1937, he suggested that a client who sought to keep costs down consider "the Territorial style as developed in various parts of the State, principally in the old part of Las Vegas," and "which we are finding from experience is cheaper to build principally because it has straighter, more conventional lines." As the Santa Fe Trail port of entry to New Mexico, Las Vegas had been a focus of American architectural influence. By 1938, Meem even designed a symmetrical, pitched roof house inspired by the imposing Baca House of Upper Las Vegas. The HABS program fell dormant in New Mexico for lack of funds from 1936 through the fall of 1939. But when Meem again put teams in the field, they focused on the Baca Residence and other Territorial examples around Las Vegas and in Santa Fe.[54]

The national ascendance of Modernism occasioned a broad aesthetic shift away from the historical revival proclivity for richly textured, natural materials, handcraftsmanship, and discrete rooms defined by solid walls. These elements gave way to a lighter pastel and white palette, smooth mass-produced glass and metal surfaces, interpenetrating interior spaces, and window walls that enhanced the visual continuity from inside to outside. Although Meem and his clients continued to favor regional historicism and handcrafted details, his palette lightened as the 1930s proceeded, while his designs also began to open from discrete rooms to flowing, interconnected spaces. Seen in this light, the Territorial Revival style, for all its regional flavor, not only lightened Meem's palette but also hid rustic wood grains under idealizing white paint and employed precise corners in keeping with the machine age. In his own house and others of the late 1930s, Meem employed blond pine vigas, in contrast to the dark, stained vigas and woodwork of earlier houses. Rather than opening out through doors, his own grand entry hall opens from floor to ceiling along one side to reveal a split staircase with views into the spaces above and below.

Because the state and university insisted on historicist designs, Meem's attempts to reconcile regionalism with Modernism during the late 1930s were limited to occasional houses. If reinforced concrete provided a satisfying substitute for massive adobe walls at the Colorado Springs Fine Arts Center, its cost and industrial associations made it unacceptable for residences. To simulate adobe, Meem had once applied colored stucco over reinforced concrete and hollow clay tile. But during the second half of the 1930s, the Modernist call for the honest use of materials increasingly entered his own rhetoric. With adobe-colored stucco over clay tile ruled out on these theoretical grounds, Meem sought ways to use traditional materials "honestly." His own house and ones for his wife's aunt, Elinor Gregg, and his office manager, Ruth Heflin, permitted him to develop an individual version of Modern Regionalism.[55]

The property he and Faith had purchased in the rolling, high desert southeast of Santa Fe included two small buildings,

La Quinta, Los Poblanos Ranch, Albuquerque (1935). (Laura Gilpin)

La Quinta portal and view east to Sandia Mountains (1935). (Laura Gilpin)

John and Faith Meem Residence
(1936). (Ernest Knee)

opposite
Gregg Residence, wall section (1939).
(*Architectural Forum*)

Elinor Gregg Residence (1939).

which he incorporated into his house design. Rather than using adobe walls or stuccoed clay tile for the new additions, Meem employed stones from the nearby arroyo, set in lime mortar like the existing structures. The similarity of the battered stone walls of his own house to the monumental stone podium of the Fine Arts Center suggests that he was continuing in a single aesthetic vein. But on the second floor, the protection afforded by a new, wraparound porch also permitted exposed earthen-plastered walls (see illustrations on p. 161).

Meem next translated this wraparound porch into projecting eaves in the 1939 Elinor Gregg Residence (see illustrations on pp. 126–127). A two-and-a-half-foot roof overhang around the entire house and a high concrete and stone foundation protected the earthen-plastered adobe walls from moisture. This pragmatic arrangement allowed traditional adobe to be displayed with the complete honesty demanded by Modernism. The single, gently sloping roof of the Gregg Residence rests on wooden decking, pole latillas, and log vigas. The latillas and vigas, of course, satisfied the picturesque desire for local, natural materials; but lacking the overt historicism of carved corbel brackets, they can be seen as elemental, structural components, arranged in a precise Modernist grid (see illustrations on p. 106).

Since the late 1920s, Meem had designed portales twelve to sixteen feet deep to function as open-air living porches. The great porch of the Gregg Residence, like most of its precursors,

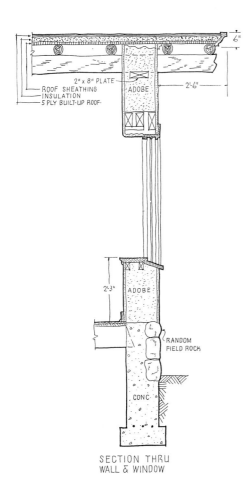

2" x 8" PLATE
ROOF SHEATHING
INSULATION
5 PLY BUILT-UP ROOF·
ADOBE
2'-6"
6"

ADOBE
2'-3"

RANDOM
FIELD ROCK

CONC·

SECTION THRU
WALL & WINDOW

orients to the best landscape views facing southwest. But because the best views for most of Meem's Santa Fe houses ranged from southeast to southwest, these living porches could also be oriented for maximum solar gain. Again, a traditional fireplace, exposed vigas, and wooden porch posts topped by carved wooden brackets contrast with the uninterrupted, Modernist flow between inside and out permitted by the porch's completely open side.

Meem again employed stone foundations, adobe walls, and projecting eaves in the 1940 Heflin Residence. Instead of a separate open-sided living porch and living room as in the Gregg Residence, he combined the two to form a living room enclosed on one side by a vast bank of windows. Its horizontal window mullions and the geometric frieze above the window echo details of the Fine Arts Center.

Many people find this attempted reconciliation unsatisfying, so contrary is the overhanging roof to the regional tradition of flat roofs with parapets. However, such a forthright attempt to overcome the nostalgia implicit in much of his work with a dynamic contemporary reinterpretation of the regional tradition is invigorating. In 1941, Meem even proposed an adobe golf course clubhouse with projecting eaves for the University of New Mexico, but university president Tom Popejoy objected that this departed from the campus style that Meem himself had defined.[56]

REGIONALISM THROUGH
WAR AND MODERNISM

The Meems' first child, Nancy, was born in April 1937. While they lived at first in the old stone buildings on the property, their new house was completed in time for the housewarming party to double as Nancy's christening celebration. In the fall of 1938, Meem was chairman of the Santa Fe Fiesta committee, and the Meems hosted the first of their annual fiestas for four hundred guests, with live music and square dancing on a platform in the house's terraced courtyard.

As Germany continued its air war against Great Britain, the Meems agreed to take four English sisters, ages six to twelve, into their home. Meem went to the East Coast to meet them and, after they arrived safely, wrote to assure their parents: "Let me tell you that I think your little girls are extraordinarily attractive and lovable. I have never seen a group that could captivate everyone's heart so readily. But these are qualities you and Mr. Mathews know *all* about. Therefore I'll not dwell on them except to say that I already love them and I know Mrs. Meem will when she sees them." For four years, Nancy and her surrogate sisters rode horses in the nearby hills and played hide and seek throughout the house.[57]

After the United States entered the war in December 1941, an intense work schedule began for the office now known as Meem & Zehner—engineer Hugo Zehner had become a partner in 1940. In eighteen months, Meem oversaw the design of base layouts, two military hospitals, and an aviators' school planned for Roswell, New Mexico—a total of twenty-five buildings, twelve million dollars of work in all, the equivalent of perhaps one hundred and fifty million today. The need for military construction on the home front ended by the summer of 1943, and Meem, a forty-seven-year-old veteran of World War I, volunteered for service. Although he lobbied for a commission with the Corps of Engineers, for whom his office had been working, Meem's recurrent migraines and other health problems blocked his induction.[58]

By the summer of 1943, as it became apparent that the Allies' victory was only a matter of time and execution, Meem and other business, government, and community leaders across the country turned their attention to plans for life after the war. In the late 1930s, Meem helped found a discussion group of twelve men, which became known as the Chili Club. Its members included George Bloom, president of the First National Bank; the painter Theodore Van Soelen; David Cole, manager of La Fonda; Paul Walter, editor of the daily *New Mexican*; Reginald Fisher, director of the Fine Arts Museum; Dan Kelly, president of the Gross, Kelly wholesale mercantile chain; pediatrician Albert Lothrop; and Father James Kingsolving of the Holy Faith Episcopal Church. Each member hosted a monthly dinner once a year and delivered a talk at a different month's meeting.

In his first talk in 1939, Meem, like other Americans, tried to imagine a way that the United States might stay out of the impending war (however, when he revisited the subject two years later, he had reconciled himself to the need to confront totalitarianism). In thirty-seven talks over the years, regional architecture was a recurrent topic, while his ongoing meditations on liberal Christian morality pervaded talks on evolution, education, politics, psychology, homosexuality, creativity, retirement, and aging.

Meem's talk for 1943 was entitled, "The Negro Problem in America." Although his title reflected contemporary thinking, Meem understood something James Baldwin would tell Americans within the following decade: The problem was not African Americans, but as Meem put it, "first and foremost, the racial arrogance of the white man." As far as he was concerned, Franz Boas, Ruth Benedict, and other anthropologists had thoroughly "disproved the myth of the master race."[59] The example of anticolonial movements in Africa and Asia, and the experience of military service, Meem thought, would cause African Americans to seek equal treatment following the war. While this would require federal initiatives, Meem challenged his discussion group: "Let's remove the unofficial, but effective taboo whereby the Negro is prevented from buying a seat on the main floor of the Lensic Theater, or occupying a room overnight in the La Fonda Hotel."[60]

Nancy and John Meem (about 1937).

At the height of the war build-up, Meem's staff had swollen to thirty-five—many worked in a plywood addition to the office. After the war, the office shrank to Meem, Zehner, and Ruth Heflin. In December 1943, Meem added Edward O. Holien, an architect trained in the Beaux-Arts tradition, who had previously worked on the design of Rockefeller Center in New York City and for Burnham Hoyt in Denver. That month, Meem also persuaded the Santa Fe Builders Supply Company (Sanbusco) to commission a group of model house plans for distribution following the war. Like the small house plans produced by Fisher & Fisher when Meem was in their Denver office, these were to be affordable two- and three-bedroom designs.[61]

These model home plans were also an exercise in futurism, Meem's projection of what life and architecture would be like following the war. Meem had gone through the process of defining a personal design idiom twice before. First, between 1925 and 1928 he had put his stamp on the Spanish-Pueblo Revival pioneered by Carlos Vierra and others. Then, between 1932 and 1934, he had created the Territorial Revival style. Now Meem attempted to define a third design mode in the title of one of these plans, "A Santa Fe Style House for Contemporary Living." As he had in defining the Territorial style, Meem began to identify and experiment with components of this new mode some years before they coalesced into a coherent idiom.

"A Santa Fe House for Contemporary Living," Sanbusco (Santa Fe Builders Supply Company) model house (1943). (Edward O. Holien)

The underlying dilemma for him remained, as it had been in the 1930s: how to continue a valued regional tradition but in an honest, modern way. Meem had confronted this dilemma most directly in his 1934 Colorado Springs Fine Arts Center and further developed his ideas in the Meem, Gregg, and Heflin Residences.

The Sanbusco commission in 1943, coming at a time when the office had virtually no other work, permitted Meem to bring this line of experimentation to fruition. His first sketched floor plans resembled the Gregg Residence layout. But, as with the Heflin Residence, the economics of middle-class houses favored the combination of the living room and solar porch. Rather than using a simple bank of windows as in the Heflin Residence, Meem now deployed a floor-to-ceiling glass curtain wall along the south side of a combined living room and dining room. The entry hall, living room, and dining room of the largest model flowed together without interruption. "The major rooms," the plan text explained, "are treated as a glass sheltered portal, tending to bring the garden and house into a unit of indoor-outdoor living." Each of the three houses was carefully laid out and sited on a typical city lot to take full advantage of passive solar heating. A cross-section drawing with each plan indicated how the December sun would penetrate deep into the living room, while the roof overhang would prevent the June sun from reaching the glass.

"Walls are of adobe," the plans explained, "protected against erosion by the over hanging viga supported roof, a treatment as characteristic historically as the more familiar parapet wall type." While some pueblos did have protective overhangings, these did not wrap around cor-

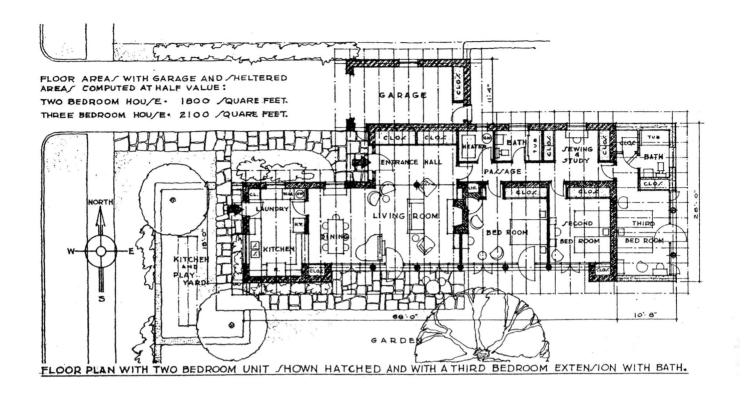

FLOOR AREAS WITH GARAGE AND SHELTERED
AREAS COMPUTED AT HALF VALUE:
TWO BEDROOM HOUSE · 1800 SQUARE FEET.
THREE BEDROOM HOUSE · 2100 SQUARE FEET.

FLOOR PLAN WITH TWO BEDROOM UNIT SHOWN HATCHED AND WITH A THIRD BEDROOM EXTENSION WITH BATH.

Sanbusco model house plan (1943).

ners and were uncommon historically compared to rounded parapets of the sort Meem used in his Spanish-Pueblo Revival designs. More important than historical precedent, Meem's intuitive grasp of the fundamental form of the time now embraced the flat, cantilevered roof forms of the International style.

During the 1930s, clay tile became more cost effective than adobe construction, joined at the end of the decade by concrete block; the two smaller plans suggested that either could be substituted for adobe. To counteract the modern look of the eaves, Meem included a few historical details: carved corbel brackets and log posts for two plans and white Territorial-style eaves and posts for the other. Windows on the north and west sides remained small, but by focusing on the east and south facades in a perspective drawing, Edward Holien emphasized the modernist expanse of glass with simple log posts and no corbel brackets. In 1944, Meem employed this emerging idiom for the Española Hospital, thirty miles north of Santa Fe.

The experience of the war profoundly affected Meem, his clients, and the new staff members he began to recruit. Some had seen combat, others lost family members. Some left farm or village for munitions work in the industrial centers, others filled jobs previously closed to them as African Americans, Hispanics, and women. Still others, like Meem, welcomed refugees into their homes and worked at a fever pitch in the war effort, but now had time to reflect on the future. The cultivation of regional traditions, which had suggested stability and continuity during the Great Depression, now seemed nostalgic—even retrograde—in light of the unavoidable international entanglements and destructive potential of modern technology that

Libby-Owens-Ford model solar house (1947).

opposite
Libby-Owens-Ford model solar house plan (1947).

the war so vividly demonstrated. The detonation of the first atomic bomb in the desert of central New Mexico in 1945, and the location of two of the nation's three nuclear weapons research labs at Los Alamos and Albuquerque, brought the new technological realities to Santa Fe's doorstep.

Within weeks of Japan's surrender in August 1945, the Libby-Owens-Ford Glass Company contacted Meem to design a prototype solar house for New Mexico. It would be reproduced in pamphlets and in a book along with designs for the other states, which included work by such architects as Pietro Belluschi (Oregon) and William Wurster (California). Meem's notes indicate the company "requested as much glass, mirrors, etc., be used in the design as compatible with our regional architecture." The nascent solar design movement in the 1940s built upon the 1930s regionalists' emphasis on local economic self-sufficiency. So Meem's design, completed in February 1946, not only would conserve energy, it also specified inexpensive local flagstone floors, adobe walls, and log roof beams. Like the Sanbusco model houses, the log eaves extended to protect the clay-plastered adobe walls, while also shading the southern windows in summer. These fixed glass curtain walls and standard metal casement windows employed the company's new double-pane insulating glass called Thermopane.[62]

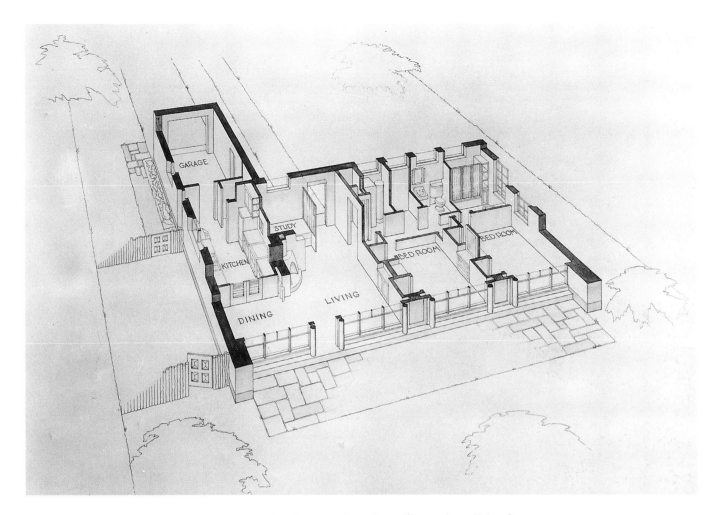

Despite the Modernist south glass curtain wall, Meem continued to utilize such traditional touches as carved corbels under the side eaves, folk Territorial doors, and corner fireplaces. As in his own house, "the pine rafters and pine board ceiling are unfinished and become increasingly beautiful with age." In the Modernist spirit, Meem further suggests that "flexibility of group living is obtained by the arrangement of living and dining spaces whereby they can be separated or thrown together." This public space also opened into an alcove beside the entrance with a built-in couch and desk, which doubled as home office and guest quarters.

Meem hoped to develop his solar house ideas with the clients who returned to him in 1945. Dr. and Mrs. W. R. Lovelace II of Albuquerque, in their conference with Meem, liked "the idea of an adobe building with projecting eaves with territorial details." But upon further reflection, they informed Meem that what they really wanted was a Territorial-style house like the one he had designed for the Robert Nordhaus family before the war. Like UNM President Popejoy, most clients who sought out Meem expected his trademark historicism.[63]

Others were uncertain about what they wanted. Meem noted after a "conference with Mr. and Mrs. L. G. Phillips in their home in Albuquerque (their young daughter was also present)," in September 1945, for instance, that "[t]he style of the house is to be preferably Spanish-

Pueblo, but all were agreed that they would like it honest. Mrs. Phillips might consider a territorial type house if it works out better." As a result, Meem produced elevation studies for both a traditional, flat-roofed Spanish-Pueblo Revival design and for a Territorial Revival house built of adobe, with an overhanging roof. When the Phillipses hesitated, Meem invited them to Santa Fe to see his and Elinor Gregg's house.[64]

The Phillipses gave their go-ahead for the projecting eave design, and the working drawings incorporated a glass curtain wall adapted from the Libby-Owens-Ford solar house plans. Instead of orienting these windows to the south for solar gain, they were placed north and east to capture views of the Sandia Mountains. In response to the plans, Mrs. Phillips wrote:

> Our daughter Mary whom you met a year ago, objects to the elevation of the north side of the living room. She thinks that the doors and windows in the glass wall should be designed to be as nearly as possible imperceptible; that if the glass wall is divided into rectangles of pleasing size, the attention will not be distracted from the view—as it is she thinks it looks a 'fussy, glassed-in porch'—as examples of the proper treatment, Mary cited the second floor of the Museum of Modern Art in New York, and a store front in Lake Placid . . . .

Meem required only a few more days than usual to reply diplomatically to Mrs. Phillips:

> I am wondering if she remembers that our approach to this house was not a strictly modern one. The detail we used is what we call "Territorial" and involves a certain number of conventional items very often associated in the east with the Greek revival or late Colonial, such as the trimmed windows, and thin painted wood columns with caps and bases. The north elevation is based on the use of a porch having the type of columns mentioned, with the porch glassed in. Miss Phillips therefore is quite correct when she claims it has a glassed-in porch although I am sorry she feels it is fussy as our effort was to make it quite simple—which I think it is. If we change the porch idea into a slab of glass, subdivided somewhat as the Modern Museum's second floor is subdivided, we really should make sure that the rest of the house won't seem out of place with its Territorial detail. It might be advisable to go completely modern.

As it turned out, a deed covenant for the subdivision where the Phillips Residence was to be built required that adobe houses be cement stuccoed within a year of completion, which prevented the "honest" use of the material. So when it was finally built in 1949, brick was substituted for adobe, although the Territorial detailing remained.[65]

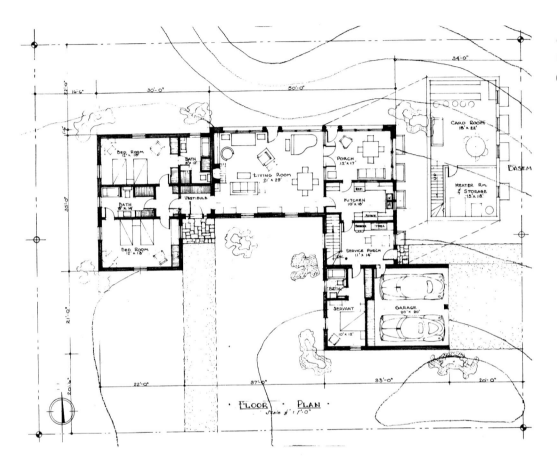

Mr. and Mrs. L. G. Phillips
Residence, Albuquerque
(1946).

FLOOR PLAN
Scale ⅜" = 1'-0"

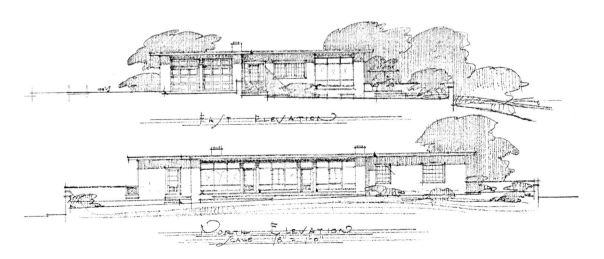

EAST ELEVATION

NORTH ELEVATION
Scale ⅛" = 1'-0"

Nancy, Faith, and John Meem
(1946). (Laura Gilpin)

In 1946 and 1947, the firm designed at least eight houses employing this "extended eaves" idiom—most with simple Territorial Revival detailing. Many of these designs went unbuilt or were modified before construction to achieve a more traditional appearance. As it turned out, most clients were interested less in the "honest" use of adobe than in a historic adobe look, whatever the underlying material. By the end of 1947, Meem abandoned his attempt to define a contemporary regional idiom. The shared sensibilities of his clients, which had been integral to the development of his two earlier idioms, were now missing. To make matters worse, he received little encouragement from other architects. The younger generation of architects schooled in doctrinaire Modernism, who staffed the burgeoning architectural offices, particularly in Albuquerque, so vehemently condemned Meem's continued use of ornament and historical symbolism that they barely noticed his solar innovations and increasingly open floor plans. (Meem was not alone among historical revival architects in his struggle to engage these broad social and artistic shifts. Leading Spanish Revival architect Wallace Neff experimented with reinforced concrete domes for defense worker housing during the war and sought to incorporate this technology in his postwar residential designs with limited success.)[66]

The outlines of America's economic and cultural dynamism following the war are well known: an industrial base untouched by war; the unleashing of human aspiration and consumer desire repressed by fifteen years of depression and war; colleges flooded by the G.I. Bill; grade schools overflowing from the baby boom; the doubling of auto ownership between 1945 and 1955, which led to suburban sprawl and the invention of the shopping mall; the explosions of bebop and abstract expressionism; the transformation of rhythm-and-blues into rock-and-roll; the rise of the civil rights movement; and, of course, the advent of television. Modernism took absolute control of the architectural journals and schools. If labor costs had been low and handcraftsmanship helped create employment during the Great Depression, labor and material costs soared in the postwar building boom. The I-beam structures and glass curtain walls of the Corporate International style—from the new United Nations building in New York to automobile showrooms across the country—now manifested mass-produced construction systems and a new techno-aesthetic.

Raymond Jonson Residence
and Gallery (1949).

Meem had begun to shift responsibility for design to Edward Holien in 1944, and, after abandoning his solar adobe house experimentation, he focused primarily on client relations and bringing in new commissions—in office parlance, he became the rainmaker. The firm of Meem, Zehner & Holien now concentrated on the design of schools, hospitals, offices, and churches. They averaged fifteen public buildings a year during the boom of the late 1940s, but a more comfortable four to five a year during the 1950s. As the university constructed seventeen new buildings in response to the enrollment explosion during the decade following the war, the regents insisted on Meem's Spanish-Pueblo Revival style. In the face of Modernism, Meem's firm was as successful as any campus architects in the country at sustaining the university's coherence by means of a simple (and relatively inexpensive) vocabulary of stepping, flat-roofed, adobe-colored, stuccoed masses. But tight budgets and breakneck schedules required simplified, sharp-edged forms and banks of mass-produced steel windows. Meem's mastery of the subtleties of picturesque composition, which added variety and a suggestion of vernacular accretion, now gave way to Edward Holien's Beaux-Arts–trained predilection for absolute symmetry. Meem had mixed cast concrete ornament with wooden details before the war at UNM, but now the firm's concrete ornamental panels lacked variety and conviction.[67]

Meem's vast knowledge of regional history and aesthetic traditions also became increasingly marginalized as the new technological aesthetic dominated even his practice. Before the war,

VIEW FROM THE SWIMMING POOL
(NORTHEAST)

SOUTH OR ENTRANCE FRONT

A · RESIDENCE · FOR · MR & MRS · ALLEN · W · HINKEL
SANTA FE, NEW MEXICO

DEC. 8, 1950

"A Residence for Mr. and Mrs. Allen W. Hinkel" (1950).

to mention but one of the many manifestations of this change, color selection was largely a matter of artistic intuition. His office formulas for custom paint colors reflected not only regional appropriateness but also firm history: not only Turquoise, Tin Roof Red, Tile Red, Spanish White, Española Dawn, and Ersatz Tierra Amarilla were used, but also Conkey House White, Andrews House Green, and Heflin Gray. After the war, Meem became a member of the AIA committee of the Inter-Society Color Council, and assembled paint manufacturers' scientifically developed color manuals for use in "color scheduling large buildings." As Faber Birren, "author of articles of functional, therapeutical and psychological aspects of color," noted in one booklet in Meem's files: "Some years ago the selection of color for most architectural projects was largely a matter of 'good taste,'. . . [but now] the architect finds himself increasingly dependent on . . . the color coordinator or functional color specialist. . . . With functional color . . . ," Faber's modernist rhetoric continues, "beauty is made subservient to utility—and pleasure becomes a by-product of purpose."[68]

Following Meem's abandonment of his solar house experimentation in 1948, the firm scaled back to only one or two houses a year. Most were designed for friends or individuals also responsible for institutional or commercial commissions. They simply wanted, in the words of one client, "that magical name—a Meem house." Meem obliged with the historical styles and design patterns he had developed before the war. John C. McHugh, a beginning architect in the firm from the late 1940s until he opened his own office in 1955, worked closely with Meem

on residential designs. Most of these designs employ a sharp-edged version of the Territorial Revival, which better suited postwar construction techniques and the persuasive technological aesthetic than sculpted adobe forms. But Meem also welcomed the opportunity in 1951 to return to his Spanish-Pueblo Revival idiom for Episcopal bishop Everett Jones and again, as he neared retirement at the end of the decade, for the McHarg Davenport and James Rogers Residences.[69]

Meem had always sought to balance his clients' desire for views with the traditional look of small pane windows framed by substantial expanses of solid wall surface. But after the war, the general desire for natural light and the kind of unobstructed picture window panoramas favored by young Miss Phillips led Meem to develop one additional residential design device. Rather than continuing the glass curtain walls of his solar house explorations, Meem simply projected the picture window outside the primary mass of a house in the form of a bay window. On the outside, this leaves a house's overall massiveness intact, while inside it produces a sunny sitting alcove. Like the informal sitting areas at one end of many of his prewar living rooms, Meem employed wall buttresses and a drop in the ceiling to articulate these alcoves, which also leave them open enough to be seen as part of the larger space.[70]

When Meem turned sixty-five in 1959, he chose to observe the conventional retirement age. "A forced or unwilling retirement," he observed in his Chili Club talk that year, "for whatever cause, is a tragedy." But one's chances of happiness improved for those who "can consciously

Proposed portal restoration, south side of plaza (1950).

control it by preparing for the change. . . . To do it successfully, two things are requisite: enough income to keep from worrying and a sufficient store of intellectual and spiritual reserves to enable him to be of service to his fellow man." Meem possessed the first and, for twenty years in retirement, actively pursued the second. He would find a measure of solace in love of family, adoration of God, and service to his community. "One's body will fail," he concluded, "one's intellect will dim, but Love can grow to the very end."

Fortunately for Santa Fe, Meem continued to make significant contributions to his community for twenty more years. He served as a board member and major supporter for such organizations as the Historic Santa Fe Foundation, the School of American Research, the Museum of International Folk Art, and the Holy Faith Episcopal Church. In 1964, Faith and John Meem were instrumental in persuading St. John's College of Annapolis, Maryland to open a new campus in Santa Fe. They donated 225 acres northeast of their house for the school, and Meem consulted with his successor firm, Holien & Buckley, on the design of its Territorial Revival–style campus. In time, the college library was named in honor of Faith and John Meem. Meem also drafted a revitalization plan for Santa Fe's plaza commercial district in 1966 and, with fellow architect Kenneth Clark, designed portales to replace those that had been removed during the Americanization of the city in the late 1800s. Meem also spearheaded the restoration of two important Territorial-era buildings—the Delgado House in 1969 and the Tully House five years later, when he was eighty years old. Nearing ninety, following bouts with cancer and depression, John Gaw Meem IV died on August 4, 1983.[71]

Meem's contributions as an architect, historic preservationist, and community leader have made his name synonymous with Santa Fe style and a commitment to regional traditions. His creative peak as a designer came between 1926 and 1941. By restraining the stage-set picturesqueness of the early Spanish-Pueblo Revival in favor of sculpted adobe masses, he brought a new gravity, elegance, and monumentality to the style. For the State Capitol complex and clients desiring formality, he developed his own brand of regional classicism—the Territorial Revival. His principled, but unsuccessful, attempt to define a contemporary Southwestern style by incorporating extended eaves and solar heating underscores the degree to which architecture is a social art dependent on supportive clients and the tenor of the times.

The greatest puzzle of Meem's architectural career is why, after having accomplished so much, he turned away from designing in his early fifties. It may have been that his health—compromised by the 1918 influenza, tuberculosis, and frequent migraine headaches—led him to the conclusion that he could not sustain his breakneck pace of the 1930s and early war years, when he carried the burden of office administration, client relations, *and* design. The pervasiveness of the techno-modernist sensibility by the late 1940s, and his inability to reconcile it with the regional tradition in a satisfactory way for his clients, probably took much of the joy out of design work. In Edward Holien, his office had an experienced designer, but one ill at ease with client relations. So, in a spirit of civic professionalism acquired from his minister father and engineer uncle, and that pervades his Chili Club meditations, Meem may have decided he could be of greatest service to his firm by focusing on administration and client relations.

The central decision of Meem's career, however, was his choice to work within a valued regional tradition, rather than trying, in the heroic Modernist mode, to overturn and transcend that tradition. He expanded stylistic idioms, adapted historic forms to contemporary needs, and invented and refined spatial design patterns. This regional tradition survived the challenge of Modernism far better than similar traditions elsewhere and has flourished again in recent decades. John Gaw Meem's greatest legacy—a legacy he shares with fellow designers and builders in and around Santa Fe—is the continuing vitality of his beloved regional tradition.

Meem in retirement (about 1980). (Sheldon Woodward)

Stairway from main portal of McCormick Residence to roof terrace, Las Acequias Ranch (1931).

PART II

DESIGN PATTERNS

Like other Beaux-Arts–trained architects of that last generation before Modernism became dogma, John Gaw Meem believed that time-tested building types and design conventions provide an appropriate starting point for new designs. In contrast to the Modernist break with history in favor of functional determinants and incessant innovation, the eclectic historicist approach gleaned social conventions and design patterns from the study of exemplary buildings and often synthesized these lessons into particular historical or regional styles.

The heyday of historical style monographs produced such books as Rexford Newcomb's *The Spanish House for America* (1927), which articulated a comprehensive design vocabulary with chapters on floor plans, exterior walls, roofs, doorways, windows, balconies, arcades, stairways, chimneys, floors and ceilings, fireplaces, furnishings, and patios and gardens. Meem's office library was filled with such books on historic and revival architecture, especially ones on Mexico, Spain, and the Spanish-Mediterranean Revival. In addition, his lifelong study of the local Pueblo and Spanish vernaculars gave him deep knowledge not only of materials and details, but also of socially and climatically adapted design forms.

One descendant of these 1920s monographs has been the coffee table book on architectural style that has appeared more frequently since 1975. They typically emphasize visual style and interior decoration, and lack any systematic engagement with deeper spatial issues—indeed, most lack floor plans. Another, more substantial descendant is the 1977 book, *A Pattern Language*, by Christopher Alexander and a group of collaborators. Like Newcomb, Alexander identifies proven design patterns, while also affording greater attention to the varying scales of human social interactions in chapters on such topics as public squares, courtyards, sequence of sitting spaces, alcoves, window places, and secret nooks for children. Likewise, in the 1990s, New Urbanism refocused attention on the value of building types, design conventions, and regional design vocabularies.

Part II examines the recurrent design patterns found in Meem's residential designs. Although informed by Pueblo, Spanish, Beaux-Arts, and picturesque eclectic traditions, Meem's use of precedent was never slavish. The adaptation of proven forms and design patterns to the needs of individual clients and the opportunities of particular building sites gave each house its unique character. This design pattern approach is not only in keeping with Meem's own thinking, it also reconstitutes a coherent regional design vocabulary with precedents and conventions of value for contemporary designers.

Dr. Dwight W. Rife Residence (1935). (Ernest Knee)

Rife Residence plan. (*Architectural Forum*)

FLOOR PLANS

John Gaw Meem drew inspiration from multistory Pueblo villages and Spanish courtyard houses. Pueblo Indians, he had observed, socialized, processed food, watched ritual dances, and even slept out on the rooftop terraces of their multistory communities. The long, narrow arms of Spanish Colonial houses also defined outdoor patios and courtyards, often completed by adjoining adobe walls. Inside the Spanish house, cooking, eating, sleeping, home craft production, and entertaining were concentrated in a single large *sala*—like the multipurpose great halls of medieval English houses.

Meem found it necessary to adapt these regional forms to the social conventions of his predominantly Anglo-American clientele. Both Meem and his clients started from the assumption that different activities would be allocated to specialized rooms, and that these would be separated into three functional clusters. At the middle would stand the public rooms—the main hall, living room, and dining room—leading to the private family quarters, and a separate service zone, including pantry, kitchen, garage, and servants' quarters.

Like other Spanish Revival architects across the Sunbelt during the 1920s, Meem adapted this Anglo organizational pattern to the courtyard form. Apart from an occasional full courtyard house, Meem opened his plans out into informal L-, U-, H-, and Y-shaped plans. The resulting narrow wings improved cross-ventilation and natural lighting. Especially in the

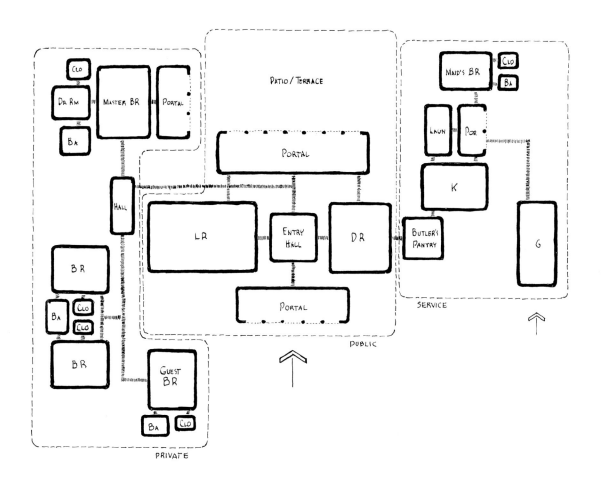

sprawling larger examples, the public, private, and service functions could be projected into separate wings. For more modest, middle-class homes, city lots with their required front- and side-yard setbacks, predicated on the compact Anglo house ideal, left less room for projecting wings and interior courtyards. The public realm was generally located near the middle of the plan because it provided circulation to the other wings. Meem took particular care to position living rooms and adjoining porches to capture landscape views and connect directly to patios, terraces, and gardens.

Most Meem-designed houses were only one story, so he had limited opportunities to employ the Pueblo roof terrace idea. When a second-floor room was included in the design, it opened directly onto a rooftop terrace. Landscape views were so important that he occasionally provided a stair solely for reaching a roof terrace if a good view could not be had on the ground level.

Typical use clusters and room adjacencies of Meem house designs. (George C. Pearl)

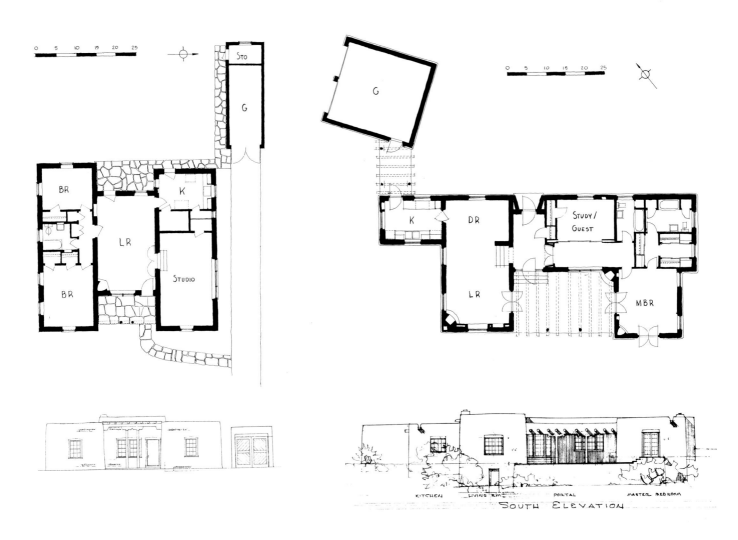

SOUTH ELEVATION

Mr. and Mrs. Kenneth Adams
Residence, Albuquerque (1939).
(Plan, George C. Pearl)

Agnes Moya Canning
Residence, Santa Fe (1953).
(Plan, George C. Pearl)

Whatever a client's budget or special requirements, Meem clustered private, public, and service functions. For Kenneth Adams, a member of the Taos Society of Artists, he adapted his H-shaped plan by turning the living room lengthwise in order to fit the house on a narrow city lot, while also placing the painter's studio where other houses had dining rooms. For Agnes Moya Canning, he augmented his earlier U-shaped Gregg House design with the sort of large,

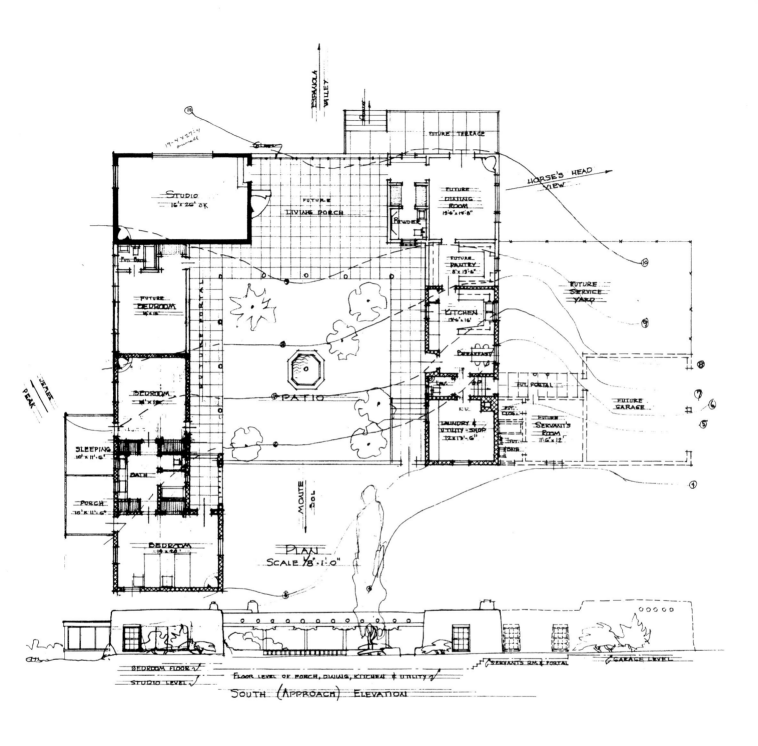

Labels visible within the plan and elevation drawings:

STUDIO 16'x26' 8K

FUTURE LIVING PORCH

FUTURE DINING ROOM 13'-6"x19'-8"

POWDER

FUTURE PANTRY 8'x13'-6"

FUTURE SERVICE YARD

KITCHEN 13'-6"x16'

BREAKFAST

FUT. PORTAL

FUTURE GARAGE

FUTURE SERVANT'S ROOM 11'-6"x12'

LAUNDRY & UTILITY SHOP 12x13'-6"

FUTURE BEDROOM 16x18

BEDROOM 14'x18'

BEDROOM 14'x18'

SLEEPING 10'x11'-6"

BATH

PORCH 10'x11'-6"

PATIO

UTILITY PORTAL

ESPAÑOLA VALLEY

HORSE'S HEAD VIEW

FUTURE TERRACE

MONTE SOL

JEMEZ PEAK

PLAN
SCALE 1/8"·1'-0"

BEDROOM FLOOR
STUDIO LEVEL
FLOOR LEVEL OF PORCH, DINING, KITCHEN & UTILITY
SERVANT'S RM. & PORTAL
GARAGE LEVEL

SOUTH (APPROACH) ELEVATION

segmented living and dining room that became popular after World War II. For conductor John Crosby, he placed the functional zones in wings wrapping a patio with views south to Monte Sol, and north from a large living porch through a glass wall to the Española Valley and Jemez Mountains—a view similar to that seen from the open air Santa Fe Opera, which Crosby would found a mile and a half to the north in 1957.

John O. Crosby Residence, preliminary plans, Santa Fe (1949). (John W. McHugh)

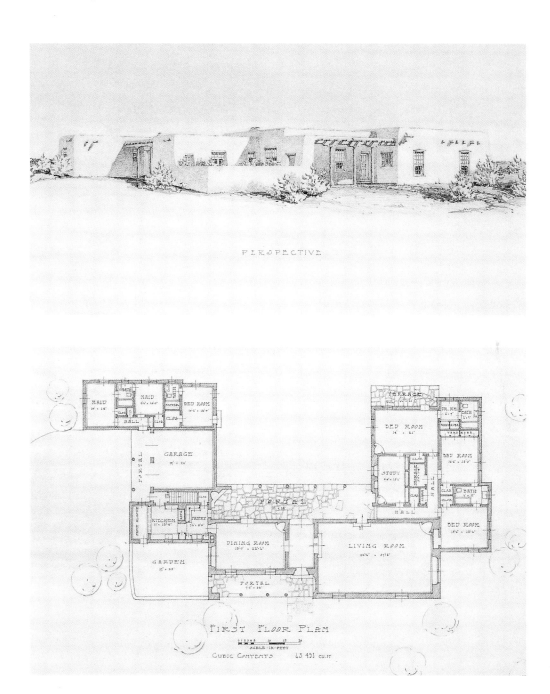

PERSPECTIVE

FIRST FLOOR PLAN

SCALE IN FEET

CUBIC CONTENTS   65 431 CU.FT

Laboratory of Anthropology Director's Residence

With a carefully balanced picturesque façade composition, an entry hall that opens on axis through a portal and garden to a view of Sunmount, and the segregation of family bedrooms and service functions into separate wings, the Laboratory of Anthropology's Director's Residence (1930) is a classic Meem design. (It is currently being adapted as a museum for the Spanish Colonial Arts Society.)

PICTURESQUE AND CLASSICAL COMPOSITION

After working through fourteen variations of one floor plan, Meem wrote to one client that "the only difficulty remaining [is] getting pleasing proportions in the main masses." But rather than employing a set geometric formula, Meem also once explained, "my method consisted merely of achieving a correct plan and then raising the ceiling to a point satisfactory to my eye." Once this had been done for each room, it was possible to rough out elevation drawings or construct a study model.

Meem sought an asymmetric, yet balanced, composition, even for modest houses. A tall living room, the shorter adjoining rooms, a somewhat shorter front porch, and even shorter garden walls provided a stepping profile. A long front porch, if given a stout masonry corner, carried sufficient visual weight to balance against the bulk of a living room. Where bedrooms and a living room framed an entry porch, the bedrooms might be projected forward a foot or two (.30 m to .61 m) to counteract the larger mass of the living room. Once the overall massing of a building was resolved, the placing of doors, windows, projecting vigas, and roof drains added variety, interest, and grace notes to the picturesque composition; Meem accentuated the rhythm of stepping masses by adding recurrent details, such as projecting roof drains. This repetition of similar forms and details gives coherence and unity to individual buildings. "When design rhymes across time," architect Douglas Kelbaugh has observed, "it demonstrates a sense of history, and when it rhymes across space, it reinforces a sense of place."

As an inexpensive way to add variety and a sense of handcraftsmanship, home builders across the country in the 1920s often used textured stucco with exaggerated trowel marks, which Meem once derided as "cheap jazz plaster effects." Meem preferred the smooth finish achieved from applying earthen plaster by hand. He simulated this on non-adobe buildings with floated cement stucco plaster. He also regretted

"Residence for Mr. and Mrs. Fredrick K. Thompson" (1929).

Meadors-Staples-Anthony Residences (1925).

opposite: McCormick Residence (1931).

that "the graceful and natural lines of erosion" characteristic of the parapet lines of traditional adobe buildings had been translated in many revival buildings "to horribly conventionalized wiggles, humps, and bumps, with a dog ear at every corner." Instead, Meem favored rounded, quietly undulating parapets, rounded corners, and moderately battered walls.

Meem's final idiom, the Contemporary Southwest, turns away from picturesque effects in favor of Modernist precision. These solar adobe houses were pulled into a single, compact mass and unified under the straight silhouette of a shed roof with extended eaves. In the most common version, adobe masses on either side of the glass curtain wall of the solar living room create a symmetrical facade.

Hollenback Residence (1932).
(Ansel Adams)

Hollenback Residence plan.
(American Architect)

Amelia Hollenback Residence

For most houses Meem simulated the balanced asymmetry and stepping masses of a multistory Pueblo village. This was a relatively easy matter if the house had a second story. Uneven hillside sites that required level changes between rooms also provided additional opportunities for stepped massing. But even for a one-story house on a level site, the tall public rooms, in particular the living room, provided the focal point for a picturesque composition, flanked by shorter, less important rooms. Pushing certain rooms away from a single uniform

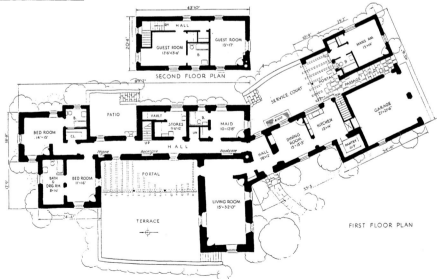

facade line also helped to vary the massing (while also increasing exterior wall surfaces, which permit windows on more than one wall for each room). The house Meem designed in 1932 for Amelia Hollenback not only evokes a picturesque Indian pueblo, it also terraces down onto stone foundations and carefully frames views of the Jemez Mountains from its west terrace. The house also incorporated a stunning collection of Spanish Colonial and Pueblo wood detailing.

Living room.

South view of Sunmount
from the living room.

View from the terrace
to the Jemez Mountains.

opposite
Terrace on the west.

Meem's Territorial Revival style, with its classical roots, called for greater formality and precision. Corners of Territorial Revival buildings were sharp instead of rounded; parapets, defined sharply by crisp brick cornices rather than undulating. Meem sometimes composed the masses of Territorial houses, such as La Quinta, symmetrically, but often varied these with minor accents. The symmetrical entry portico of the Tilney Residence, for instance, is balanced on either side by wings that at first seem symmetrical but, on closer inspection, turn out to have been subtly varied in mass and window locations in response to interior functions. Where asymmetry was employed, in the John Simms Residence for instance, the entry porch and screened porch were nevertheless carefully balanced on either side of the living room mass.

North facade of La Quinta, Los Poblanos Ranch, Albuquerque (1935).

John F. Simms Residence, Albuquerque (1935).

ENTRY PATHS

A well-designed entrance is identified easily by approaching visitors and offers shelter from the elements. The eye-catching details of a Spanish- or Territorial-style portal satisfy the first need; a porch roof surrounded on two or three sides by the house satisfy the second. But an entrance is also a threshold for social encounters. It can define the end of a long journey or mark the beginning, ending, or resumption of a relationship. John Gaw Meem developed a variety of devices to ennoble the social rituals of arrival and departure; in his finest examples, he elongated entry paths into richly nuanced sequences of impressions and pausing places.

Meem's entry sequences extended from the edge of a property to the front door, through an entry hall and living room, and out to a courtyard, patio, or terraced garden. Given his affinity for picturesque aesthetics, they resemble the winding pathways of an English garden with carefully planned series of glimpsed, then obscured, then fully revealed vistas, of architectural follies, sitting places, and picturesquely composed scenes.

While the organization of Meem's entry sequences was picturesque and winding, most included passages of axial formality: frequently the approach to the main entry or a porch or garden focused on a distant peak. Meem articulated a series of thresholds along these paths by means of steps, massive adobe piers topped by cross beams at the end of porches, ornate entry doors with side lights and transoms, and changes in ceiling heights and floor surfaces, especially where a path turns ninety degrees. Strung along these paths, like a collection of exotic stones and beads on a knotted brown cord, are what Meem, his clients, and architectural magazines referred to as "features." A flagstone or brick floor, an antique door or railing, a framed view of a garden or distant landscape, the beams and carved brackets of a porch or living room ceiling, a fireplace flanked by built-in adobe benches, and wall niches designed to receive a Pueblo pot or carved *santo*—all qualified as features of interest to be placed judiciously along the path in the neutral setting of simple adobe walls.

The interaction of tourism promotion and Hollywood set design with the Spanish Revival in California fostered the use of scenographic devices in house design. In *The Spanish House for America*, for instance, Rexford Newcomb describes the series of enticing views visible from the public rooms of one house, including "the splendid vista obtained from the dining-room when one looks out through the doorways and through the arch at the end of the *portal* (porch) to the low, parapeted terrace beyond." Images of romantic Spanish courtyards and Indian pueblos attracted tourists and many of Meem's clients to New Mexico so it is not surprising to find similar qualities in Meem's work. Photographs taken by Ansel Adams and Laura Gilpin of Meem's finished houses record layered wall planes punctuated by doors and windows that offer glimpses of stairways, sculpted fireplaces, balconies, and landscape views—all evoke the romance of the Southwest.

The Berkeley Johnson Residence

The entry sequence of a middle-class home such as the 1935 Berkeley Johnson Residence might include a gently curving flagstone sidewalk leading to a portal, a framed glimpse of a garden wall at the end of this porch, a heavy front door with a wrought-iron grill over its small window, a similar door to the vestibule coat closet, a diagonal view across a living room to a sculpted fireplace, and, finally, a view from the dining room out to the backyard patio and garden.

Las Acequias—The McCormick Residence

The McCormicks's trip each summer from Chicago to Las Acequias, their "small vacation establishment" north of Santa Fe, was a cinematic experience. Mimbres-style china in the dining car of the Super Chief and Mission-style passenger depots announced the Southwest even before the tall grass Great Plains gave way to sagebrush mesas and glimpses of the distant Rocky Mountains. After a pause at La Fonda on the Santa Fe plaza—with its recent additions by Meem—they drove the final eighteen miles over gravel, then dirt roads snaked through the verdant Tesuque valley, up over bone-dry badlands with the Sangre de Cristos looming to the east, and finally into the Rito Pojoaque valley. Turning onto their one-hundred acre (4047 sq m) estate, the McCormicks wound down a narrow, cottonwood-lined lane past lush pastures, lily-covered irrigation ponds, and timeworn adobe houses. Passing between two old farmhouses—which were converted by Meem into guest cottages—the McCormicks arrived in the forecourt of their sprawling, adobe summer house, with a panorama of the Sangre de Cristos opening to the east.

Winding approach to McCormick Residence and the view east from the visitor's cottage, Las Acequias Ranch.

Man's BR
Maid's BR
Auto Court
Laun
Nook
Desert Garden
K
DR
Sto
Studio
Clo
BR
Garden
Ba Dr
Boudoir
Study
Sun R
Terrace
LR

0 5 10 15 20 25

McCormick Residence plan (1931),
including the sun room addition
of the late 1940s. (George C. Pearl)

opposite
East facade.
Sun room.
Southeast corner.

They entered through a pair of heavy old wooden doors, and descended a long portal that steps down the hillside through the heart of the house—a spine with rooms, porches, and views opening on either side. First on the left, a small desert garden of yuccas, prickly pear cactus, scraggly piñon pine, and a distant glimpse of Pecos Baldy peak. Through another pair of heavy doors and a small entry hall, this descending path reaches a pivotal juncture. To the right, a porch opens to a garden overlooking fields and cottonwoods. Ahead, the portal continues on axis to the living room. Diagonally to the left lies a lush terraced garden with a view across the valley. And directly to the left, a long portal leads to the bedroom wing and, in an earlier plan, to a shuttered opening, overlooking the desert hillside and a final panorama of the Sangre de Cristos (see illustrations on p. 31).

opposite

Entrance portal looking north to auto court.

Entrance portal double corbel bracket.

Ceiling at crossing of main portales.

Portal to living room, enclosed after original construction.

Portal to bedroom wing opening to brick terrace.

East terrace and
living-room portal.

West garden with
glimpse of maids' portal.

Irrigated field and apple
orchard south of house.

opposite
View from east terrace over
irrigated fields to the Sangre
de Cristos.

Laboratory of Anthropology Director's Residence.

SALAS AND LIVING ROOMS

John Gaw Meem's primary clients were doctors, lawyers, politicians, businessmen, and civic women; they not only entertained close friends but also hosted receptions for professional and community groups, which required a formal living room that could comfortably accommodate thirty or more people. The rectangular American living room originated from the multipurpose, medieval English hall and a regional precedent in the Spanish sala. New Mexican salas were limited by available timber to widths of 16 ft (4.88 m) or so, although these were often stretched to 25 ft (7.62 m) or so in length, with ceilings 8 to 10 ft (2.44 to 3.05 m) tall. Meem typically enlarged these dimensions to 16 to 18 ft (4.88 to 5.49 m) in width, 30 or more ft (9.1 m) in length, and 9 to 10 ft (2.74 to 3.05 m) in height.

Regularly spaced vigas, often resting on carved brackets, unified the space. Ornate ceilings and large adobe fireplaces also imparted regional character. In slightly more than half of his living room designs, Meem adopted the Anglo-American mid-wall, rectangular fireplace. New Mexico residents mainly opted for these formal fireplaces, while those building summer vacation homes more often embraced the Spanish-style corner fireplace. Meem also followed the Spanish practice of projecting a small wing wall from one of the long sides of the room to receive a corner fireplace—a design that brings the heat source nearer the middle of the room. In either case, a fireplace positioned strategically near the middle of the room provides an architectural backdrop for after-dinner talks and rounds of toasts.

A living room inevitably also serves smaller gatherings and day-to-day family life. Families defined these smaller social circles through their furniture arrangement. The fireplace was usually the focus for a symmetrical grouping of one or two couches and as many overstuffed chairs. A window seat, alcove, and, in a few instances, a second fireplace suggested a location for a more informal furniture grouping. Meem anticipated these likely furniture groupings by positioning doors so that traffic might flow easily around them.

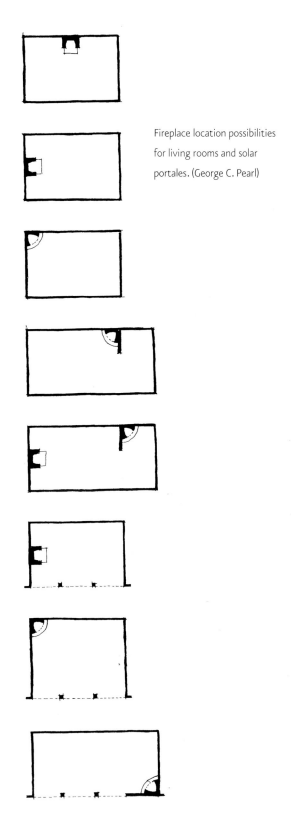

Fireplace location possibilities for living rooms and solar portales. (George C. Pearl)

Los Poblanos, Albuquerque.
(Laura Gilpin)

McCormick Residence, studio
remodeled into living room by
Meem around 1950.

Amelia Hollenback Residence.

Laboratory of Anthropology
Director's Residence.

Conkey Residence.

The size and shape of dining rooms were even more emphatically linked to their primary function: seating eight or ten people around a rectangular or oval table. Meem's dining rooms are generally 13 or so ft (3.96 m) wide, and 17 or so ft (5.18 m) long. Most also have a corner fireplace; about half, a built-in china cabinet. In some summer residences, and in modest houses designed after 1935, a separate formal dining room was dispensed with in favor of a dining area located at one end of the living room.

McCormick Residence, candle-lit as originally intended by the McCormicks.

Ballroom at La Quinta, Albuquerque (1935). (Laura Gilpin)

Conkey Residence (1928).

Meem Residence (1937).

Window seats, from the top: The first Brownell-Howland Residence (1930); John Simms Residence (1935); McHarg Davenport Residence (1951); Everett Jones Residence (1958); Laboratory of Anthropology Director's Residence (1930). (George C. Pearl)

opposite
John Simms Residence (1935).

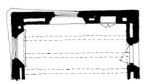

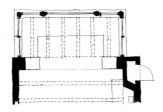

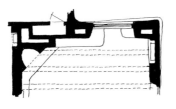

ALCOVES AND WINDOW SEATS

Alcoves and window seats abound in Meem houses—places for three or four people to chat over tea or drinks, for two to have an intimate conversation, and for a solitary individual to read a novel, while lifting his or her eyes occasionally to gaze into a garden or out across the distant landscape.

Set into thick adobe walls, a seat 18 in (45.72 cm) deep, 30 in (76.2 cm) wide, and 17 in (43.18 cm) tall allows a person to sit comfortably parallel to a window. Meem sometimes shaped the splayed reveals of windows to fit the curve of a person's back. A window seat 6 or 8 ft (1.83 or 2.44 m) in length accommodates two. By pushing a bench outside a building's solid walls, and wrapping it with glass on three sides, Meem also created bay windows. Deepening this into an alcove 5 or 6 ft (1.52 or 1.83 m) deep accommodates a U-shaped bench. In addition to the attraction of views and natural light, Meem often placed a radiator under window seats for added winter comfort.

Master bedroom, James R. Cole Residence (1947). (Laura Gilpin)
Los Poblanos.

Meem also articulated alcoves at the ends of living rooms in a variety of ways. At Las Acequias, the McCormicks' summer place, he created an alcove two steps above the living room with perpendicular beams and its own fireplace. At Los Poblanos, the Simms's Albuquerque ranch house, the alcove is level with the living room but has a lower ceiling, is narrower, and, again, has its own fireplace and perpendicular beams. In the Conkey residence near Sunmount, a stem wall, and Spanish fireplace, divides the living room into unequal parts, with a large window seat giving character to the smaller portion. At 7 to 10 ft (2.13 to 3.05 m) deep, and 16 or so ft (4.88 m) wide, these alcoves are often large enough to be rooms. But while they foster small social clusters, they also link visually with the main living room space to accommodate overflow gatherings.

The presence of a fireplace, by itself, implies a social hearth —at the least, a sitting area with a couch or a pair of chairs, a side table, and lamp. Meem provided for sitting areas in bedrooms, for instance, by adding a corner fireplace and lengthening the room 4 or 5 ft (1.22 to 1.52 m) beyond what was needed for beds and dressers. Indeed, the provision of fireplaces, window seats, and built-in adobe benches (*bancos*), and the positioning of doors to route traffic around the adjoining space created prospective social islands, which owners brought to life by adding furniture. Two or three chairs and a low table pulled up to a long window seat, a family's heirloom tea service on a serving tray or cart, and a genteel hostess are all that is needed for the ritual of afternoon tea.

When architecture is combined with furniture, social custom and family habits create a varied sequence of social areas in Meem houses: a wooden bench under the entry porch; a window seat in an alcove flanked by two chairs; a couch and easy chairs around a fireplace; a pair of easy chairs beside a bedroom fireplace; and a bench tucked in the corner of the garden. Meem wrote this reminder following a conference with one client: "[P]rovide as many terraces, portales, and nooks as possible so as to make the whole interesting in appearance and inviting to lounge in."

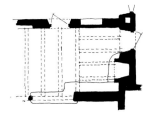

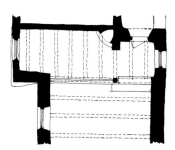

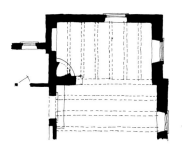

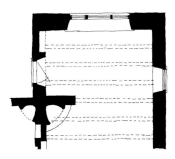

Alcoves, from top: Laboratory of
Anthropology Director's Residence (1930);
McCormick Residence (1931);
Los Poblanos (1932);
Conkey Residence (1928). (George C. Pearl)

Laboratory Director's Residence.

In only a handful of cases—Meem's own house, for one—is the kitchen large enough to accommodate a table and chairs as traditional farm kitchens had. In most of his designs, the heat, smells, and noise generated by servants preparing meals were buffered from the dining room by a pantry and swinging doors. Meem departed from the prevailing utilitarian aesthetic of the 1920s in a few kitchens when he employed stove hoods and alcoves lined with colorful Mexican tiles. The examples of Spanish Revival houses in California undoubtedly encouraged Meem and his clients to look for inspiration to the colonial kitchens of Mexico. For smaller houses, the home economics movement early in the twentieth century fostered an image of the kitchen as a sanitary, efficient food production space, where housewives took the place of servants. But by the 1930s a desire for the old-fashioned social kitchen led to the popularity of breakfast nooks—a device Meem especially employed for smaller houses.

The revived desire for social kitchens, along with the disappearance of servants, and the availability of fresh produce year-round after World War II, has made the kitchen the most frequently remodeled room in older houses. In Meem houses, the old pantry or a kitchen porch has often been combined with the original kitchen to produce a room large enough to accommodate the ever-expanding number of modern appliances and provide a place for the family to eat together.

McCormick Residence (1931).

Laboratory of Anthropology Director's Residence (1930).

opposite

Meem Residence (1937).

FIREPLACES

A fire glowing at the heart of a home and the opportunity to lose oneself in the hypnotic flicker of the flame or to join a convivial gathering around the hearth—such are the promises of the fireplace for the Arts and Crafts movement and its enclave centered at Santa Fe. "If I had my way," wrote Meem to one client, "I would put a fireplace in every room." Two of his houses—Las Acequias and the first Brownell-Howland Residence—each have nine, although most Meem houses have one each in the living and dining rooms and one or two in bedrooms. Even one-room guest cottages had one. It is impossible to speak of Santa Fe style without speaking of fireplaces.

Pueblo Indians and their Anasazi ancestors generally placed fires, whether in dwelling rooms or in ceremonial kivas, on a stone hearth under a smoke hole in the middle of the ceiling. Spanish colonists who arrived in 1598 introduced the fireplace to the Southwest. Known in local parlance as a *fogón*, these corner fireplaces are made of adobe, quarter round in plan, with hearths raised 6 in (15.24 cm) or so above the floor, an elliptical opening perhaps 20 in (50.8 cm) tall, and a square flue rising above a curved mantel. With fireboxes only 18 in (45.72 cm) or so deep, small logs or split kindling are burnt vertically but radiate surprising warmth. (Although often referred to as *kiva fireplaces* today, this is a misnomer because it misattributes the cultural origins of the fireplace.)

Dining room, Conkey Residence (1928).
Dining room, Meem Residence (1937).

opposite
Bedroom, Conkey Residence.

In large, rectangular salas the fireplace was often placed near the middle of one long wall at a 3- to 4-ft (92- to 1.22-m) wing wall; this stem wall, a *paredcito* (meaning little wall, the letters are transposed by some to yield *padrecito*, little father), might also form a windbreak for the entrance door. Meem employed both corner and paredcito fireplaces. Those located in bedrooms were about the size of historic examples, although Meem made those in living and dining rooms larger to provide a suitable focus for these public rooms.

In houses with modern heating systems, fireplaces went unused much of the time. In compensation, Meem, like other Santa Fe designers, made his fireplaces into sculptures in their own right. Curved faces and stepping wing buttresses projecting out along either wall echo the rounded, stepping profiles of mesas, of Pueblo villages, and of the garden walls of many Meem houses. Raised flagstone or brick hearths, painted dados arching around the fireplace opening, and wrought-iron damper handles added further interest. One- and two-tiered mantels, wall niches flanking chimneys, and paredcitos that step down gracefully provide the settings for Pueblo pots, Apache baskets, carved Spanish *santos*, and tinwork candelabras. Flanked by built-in adobe bancos and positioned in an alcove, these fireplaces became the regional equivalent of the Arts and Crafts inglenook fireplace.

Beginning in the 1850s, the U.S. Army and Anglo-American newcomers introduced a new type of fireplace to the Southwest—one located in the middle of and flush with the wall, with a projecting mantel, a rectangular opening, and a hearth flush with the floor. Although often lined inside with fired brick shipped over the Santa Fe Trail, they were typically built

Library at La Quinta (1935). (Laura Gilpin)
La Quinta.

opposite
Living room, Conkey Residence.

Meadors-Staples-Anthony
Residences (1925).
McHarg Davenport Residence (1951).

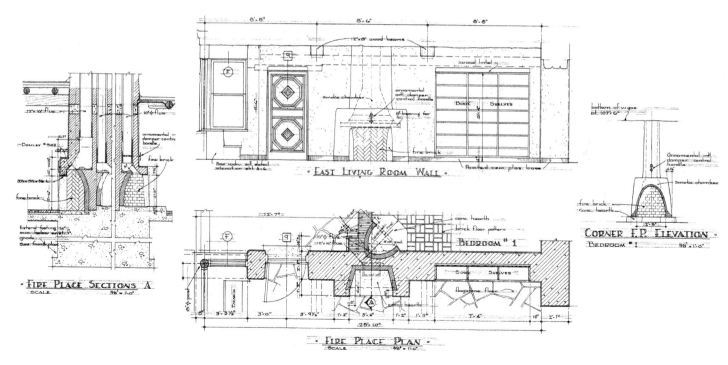

of the most readily available material—adobe. Recently established sawmills provided lumber that carpenters worked into ornamental mantels and surrounds. Meem replicated historic mantels, evocative of Federal and Greek Revival mantels in the East, for his Territorial Revival houses and for clients who desired particular formality in their libraries, living rooms, and dining rooms.

So strong was the predilection of many clients for the Anglo-style, mid-wall fireplace—even before the emergence of the Territorial Revival in the 1930s—that Meem designed adobe, mid-wall fireplaces for Spanish-Pueblo Revival houses. Sometimes these had wooden mantels with the regional inflection of a carved cord molding—a decorative motif employed by Franciscan missionaries, whose rope belts symbolized their vow of poverty. In most cases, however, Meem projected mid-wall fireplaces out to create an adobe mantel. The flue might also project from the wall, while an elliptical opening and stepping buttresses sometimes created an even more picturesque effect. On other occasions, Meem recessed the fireplace into the wall under a carved beam to form a recess mantel or inglenook.

Berkeley Johnson Residence (1935).
Elinor Gregg Residence (1939).

CEILINGS, FLOORS, AND WALLS

Ceilings and floors provide the best opportunities for the display of rustic materials, hand-craftsmanship, and ornamental details. They give character to individual rooms, while also establishing a visual hierarchy within the house. By comparison, the primary aesthetic role of interior walls in Meem houses, and more generally in Santa Fe–style homes, is to provide a neutral setting for the richness of floors and ceilings and for the residents' Southwestern, contemporary, and regional folk art collections. Most walls are hard plastered and painted a light brown or cream color, although a few are finished with traditional earthen plaster.

In Pueblo and Spanish Colonial New Mexico, ceilings were built simply of log beams, known as vigas, overlaid with small pole latillas, and finished with a layer of grass and another of earth. Carved ornamental wooden corbels placed under the vigas and atop porch posts were reserved for churches and the homes of the well-to-do. Meem made extensive use of such carved wooden brackets on entry porches and in entry halls, living rooms, and dining rooms. His bedroom ceilings were typically simple log vigas without carved brackets or plaster ceilings, which were also specified for kitchens and bathrooms.

Spanish Colonial ceilings reused in the Hollenback Residence (1932).

Top, from left; Conkey Residence (historic ceiling), McCormick Residence (historic ceiling), Meem Residence.

Middle: Laboratory Director's Residence, Meem Residence, McCormick Residence (historic ceiling).

Bottom: Gregg Residence, Gregg Residence, Laboratory Director's Residence.

For his Territorial Revival houses, Meem employed plaster ceilings with cove moldings for major rooms and, in a few cases, whitewashed milled beams with rough-sawn decking. Because Meem's architecture was predominantly flat-roofed, open wooden trusses topped by heavy exposed beams appear only in the occasional California Ranch–style house.

Historic New Mexican floors were usually finished with adobe mortar and clay and, at least according to legend, with ox blood, added for resilience; occasionally, with flagstone; and, only rarely, with wooden planks. Meem sometimes simulated adobe floors with painted concrete and, in a few cases, employed leathery brown mastic—a commercial flooring product made of ground brick or powdered lime mixed with a tar-based cement. For porches and entry halls, he favored flagstone and fired bricks, then popular in Spanish Revival homes. But as he explained to one supplier, "I am trying to get an old fashioned, rather primitive effect with fire flashed, rather dark burned bricks, with slight irregularities in color and shape."

Bricks turned perpendicular to the walls create a border around herringbone and basket weave patterns and, some-

Laboratory Director's Residence.

From left: McCormick Residence, Johnson Residence, Meem Residence.

times, ornamental variations set in an overall grid. But for bedrooms and many living rooms and dining rooms, Meem felt his clients were "more comfortable with the wood than they would be with a more appropriate material such as concrete or flagging." In kitchens and bathrooms, where hygiene and ease of cleaning were paramount, he typically specified terra-cotta tiles or linoleum.

In his material selection and detailing of ceiling, floor, and wall materials, Meem expressed a hierarchy of importance and use unknown in the Pueblo and Spanish traditions but analogous to the hierarchy of door, ceiling, and fireplace mantel moldings and other details in American colonial houses and classical Beaux-Arts design. Thick walls that resulted in deep door and window reveals gave weight to entry halls and living and dining rooms, further accentuated by carved ceilings and large fireplaces. Heavy traffic areas, especially the transitions into the house, received long-wearing flagstone and fired brick. Transitions in the entry sequence, and from room to room, were further articulated by changes in floor materials, ornamental borders, and intervening steps. Likewise, a right-angle shift of the orientation of ceiling beams from one room to the next accentuated changes in use or in direction of entry.

Hollenback Residence.

Laboratory Director's Residence.

opposite
McCormick Residence.

DOORS

Concentrated bursts of ornament set in broad expanses of plain walls typify New Mexican colonial architecture, like that of Mexico and Spain. Builders in central Mexico and Spain often framed their entries with elaborately carved stone reliefs; those in New Mexico with their more limited skills and rudimentary tools concentrated their ornamentation on the door itself (and during the Territorial era on paneled reveals). Their modest approximations of Spanish frame-and-panel doors consisted of vertical stiles on the sides, horizontal rails at the top and bottom, and one or more stiles or rails subdividing the frame. Mortised and tenoned together, these elements defined rectangles, filled with hand-adzed wooden panels. For window grills and shutters, New Mexican carpenters generally resorted to two-dimensional, cut-out approximations of lathe-turned spindles.

After milled lumber and carpentry tools became more widely available following the Civil War, carpenters—especially in mountain villages such as Truchas, Peñasco, and Chacon—elaborated the local Spanish door tradition into an exuberant folk art. They sometimes finished their doors, which were of vertical planks butted together, by nailing simple Z-braces on one or both sides as carpenters did elsewhere. Many New Mexican carpenters instead employed board frames resembling the Spanish door frames, not mortised and tenoned together, but nailed to the front and, sometimes, the back of the planks to form two- and three-ply doors. While this outside frame and its internal subdivisions create two or more shallow rectangular compartments, the application of small wood blocks in the corners of these compartments produces cross forms—a sign of deep Catholic devotion.

Territorial-era door,
Hollenback Residence.

opposite
top: Territorial-era and Spanish
Colonial doors, Hollenback
Residence.

bottom left: Hollenback Residence

bottom right: Laboratory Director's
Residence.

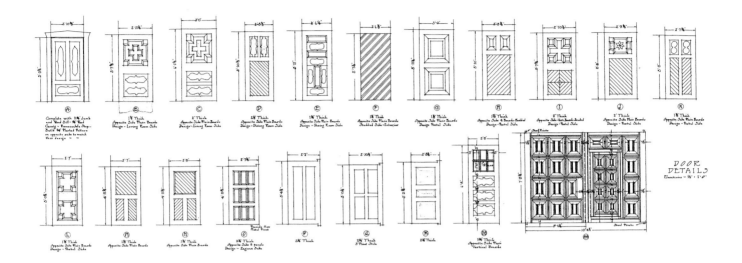

Working with a handsaw, a miter box for making angled cuts, and one or two molding planes, which shaped the edges of boards into curving profiles, carpenters trimmed these cross-shaped and rectangular recesses with pieces of wooden molding, vertical or diagonal boards, paired cut-out brackets, and hand-carved star and floral motifs. Folk Territorial carpentry in isolated villages only waned on the eve of the First World War, just as the regional revival commenced in Santa Fe.

left to right: Los Poblanos, Johnson
Residence; La Quinta, La Quinta;
La Quinta, Gregg Residence.

opposite
Vegetable garden gate, Proctor
Residence (1929), contemporary
reproduction by John Gaw Meem
Designs (James Hart Photograph),
reproduction by John Gaw Meem
Designs (James Hart Photograph),
Cristo Rey Church (1939), reproduc-
tion by John Gaw Meem Designs
(James Hart Photograph).

Spanish-Pueblo Revival–buildings in the teens and early twenties employed simple Spanish frame and panel doors, or rustic Mission-style plank doors. In one of Meem's early houses—the Meadors Residence of 1926—he designed plank doors with Z-braces fastened with modern screws and washers, arranged to recall the ornamental patterns of hand-wrought nails on Spanish and Mexican doors. Other Meem clients desired Spanish Revival frame doors elaborated with heavy moldings.

But Meem also knew the Territorial doors of the high mountain villages, and some of his clients collected antique doors for use in their houses. The four Spanish Colonial frame doors, a pair of small doors for an *alacena* (built-in cabinet), and the fifteen folk Territorial doors collected in 1929 by Misses Brownell and Howland, provided an exceptional catalog of regional doors. All but one of these doors was less than 6 ft (1.83 m) tall; five of them measured only 5 ft (1.52 m) in height. To make them serviceable, Meem mounted them over 6- to 9-in (15- to 23-cm) tall, raised doorsills. Meem also adapted motifs from these doors for such modern necessities as radiator covers. For example, one radiator cover in the living room of the Brownell-Howland Residence, echoes the alacena doors mounted in the wall nearby, while another cover repeats the bracket motif of the antique door at its side.

Territorial doors were not only smaller than contemporary doors, they also tended to expand, contract, and warp—a problem exacerbated when they were installed in houses with central heating, which increased the variation of temperature from inside to out. The rise of central heating was also accompanied by increased expectations of an airtight house. As a result, Meem translated the nailed-on frame designs of the three-ply doors back into true frame-and-panel doors, less given to warping.

While the bracket, cross, and diagonal board motifs of the Brownell-Howland doors appeared again and again in subsequent work, Meem also developed his own designs in the spirit of the Spanish- and Territorial-era carpenters. At the top of one garden door, he metamorphosed the two-dimensional, cut-out spindles of Spanish times into zigzag Pueblo lightning motifs, while below he employed the Territorial diagonal board motif but with the corners omitted to create triangular recesses.

If oiled and left unpainted as in Spanish times, the wood grain adds to the rustic quality of the door. But by painting many of his doors white in the Territorial manner, Meem emphasized the handcraftsmanship of the moldings and the carefully designed geometric patterns, which yielded patterns of light and shadow.

Entrance door with side lights echoed by porch door, Gregg Residence.

Living-room wall drawings for Brownell-Howland Residence (1930), with radiator cover based on adjoining Spanish Colonial cabinet doors.

opposite
top left: Meem adopted the Territorial-era practice of wrapping doors with side lights and transoms that are adorned with pedimented lintels, Meem Residence.

top right and bottom: At La Quinta, the John Simms Residence, and Los Poblanos, Meem similarly adapted the motifs of historic doors and window grills to wrap radiators.

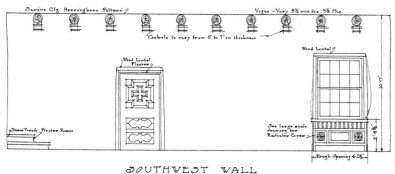

SOUTHWEST WALL

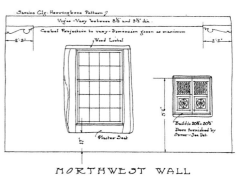

NORTHWEST WALL

BUILT-INS

The shortage of metal carpentry tools in colonial New Mexico meant that freestanding furniture was limited. Instead, builders incorporated adobe bancos, wall niches, and built-in shelves in their houses. In Meem's own day, the Arts and Crafts movement, as demonstrated in the space-saving Craftsman bungalow, favored all manner of built-ins: bookshelves, china cabinets, breakfast nooks, medicine cabinets, fold-out ironing boards, fold-up Murphy beds, larger closets than in Victorian-era houses, and California cooler closets with air vents to the outside for refrigerating food in winter.

In addition to window seats and adobe benches, Meem often included built-in china cabinets in his dining rooms, wall niches throughout his houses, and extensive built-in bookshelves in his living rooms or libraries. The colorful spines of books standing flush with the wall surface, often framed by wood trim, became a notable visual feature—one that displayed the owner's interests and erudition. Many bookcases were positioned to enhance the importance of fireplaces by either symmetrically flanking a formal fireplace or offering an asymmetric complement to a paredcito fireplace.

opposite
Laboratory Director's Residence.

Los Poblanos.
Living room, Meem Residence.

View from entry hall to living room, Conkey Residence.

Like other architects of the Spanish Revival movement, Meem concentrated his closets and built-ins in interior walls. A conventional pairing of closets between bedrooms, for instance, provided sound buffering. Likewise, a coat closet and a shallow cabinet facing an entry hall, and bookcases facing the adjoining living room, created a thick wall and an unusually deep door reveal between the two rooms. If necessary, to achieve this massive adobe affect, Meem simply hollowed cavities within his walls.

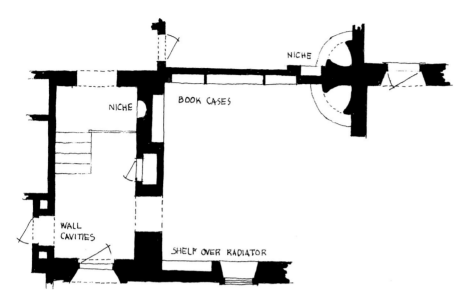

The design of electric light fixtures compatible with Meem's rustic Spanish-Pueblo style required particular care. He encouraged the use of wall sconces or table and standing lamps for most principal rooms so as not to compete with their elaborate carved wooden ceilings. Because local historic iron and tin work had been modest, Meem and his staff drew inspiration from books in his office library on Mexican and Spanish metal fixtures to design octagonal iron or tin hanging chandeliers for dining rooms with plaster ceilings, and octagonal lanterns for portales and entry halls. Wrought-iron work, so prevalent in the pure Spanish Revival of the 1920s, is limited in Meem's residences to the occasional stair railing or garden gate.

Plan of built-ins of the entry hall and living room of the Conkey Residence (1928).

John Simms Residence.
La Quinta.
Meem Residence.
Meem Residence.

SOLAR PORTALES AND LIVING PORCHES

New Mexicans traditionally created outdoor living spaces adjoining their residences. Multi-story Pueblo villages, and those of their Anasazi ancestors, typically turned blank walls to the cold northwestern wind, thereby sheltering roof-top terraces stepping down to the southeast. Likewise, Spanish and Mexican builders wrapped their L- and U-shaped houses around south-facing portales (porches) and courtyard patios.

By contrast, many early-twentieth-century newcomers to Santa Fe simply applied adobe styling to compact house plans more appropriate to the climates of their native Midwest or Northeast. John Meem's childhood in Brazil, by comparison, made him more attuned to the deeper spatial patterns of the New Mexican vernacular, and he typically opened out his plans to create sheltered courtyards and terraces. But the location of Santa Fe and Taos at 7,000 ft (2137 m), and Albuquerque at 5,000 ft (1524 m), meant these outdoor rooms were only comfortable six or eight months of the year.

PORTAL LOOKING PAST FRONT DOOR TO BEDROOM WING

F. G. Coates Residence (about 1954). (John W. McHugh)

opposite
Laboratory Director's Residence.

As a result, Meem retrofitted the portales of his earliest houses with window inserts for winter, while in houses designed after about 1928, he incorporated full-blown solar portales—deep porches oriented south or southeast toward the rising sun. If Spanish Colonial portales had typically been 6 or 8 ft (183 m or 244 m) deep, Meem now made his solar porches 12, 15, or even 18 ft (3.66, 4.57, or 5.4864 m) deep, and 25 ft (7.62 m) wide—the dimensions of a sala. Multiple doors connect adjoining rooms to this new center of activity. A brick or flagstone floor over a concrete slab provides thermal mass to absorb the winter sun, while a roof projecting 18 to 24 in (46 to 61 cm) beyond the edge of the porch leaves it shaded at the height of summer.

Entirely open on one side, Meem equipped most solar portales with a fireplace to augment the warmth of the winter sun. Many also have glass panels that are removable in summer or permanent windows with multiple French doors that can be thrown open on temperate days. Meem's earlier and larger houses have both a formal living room and what his drawings term a "living portal." But by the second half of the 1930s, fully glazed solar portales began to double as living rooms, especially in more modest homes. If Meem's fireplaces with built-in adobe bancos echo Arts and Crafts inglenook fireplaces, his solar portales provide a new, sun-drenched form of social hearth for the home.

McLane Residence, Colorado Springs (1932). (Chris Wilson)
Mrs. P. G. Cornish Residence, Albuquerque (1948). (Laura Gilpin)
McCormick Residence (1931).
Los Poblanos (1932).

opposite
Los Poblanos.

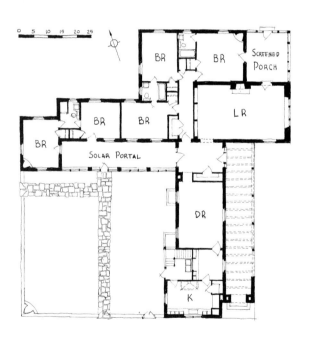

John F. Simms Residence

Designed in 1935 for John Simms, this house incorporates a handsome entry portal, screened-in porch, and solar portal, while also sheltering a courtyard completed by a waist-high wall (see also illustrations on p. 75). (The plan shows Meem's design, which was modified in construction.) Simms was an influential attorney and later New Mexico Supreme Court justice, whose brother, Albert, and sister-in-law, Ruth Simms, developed the nearby Los Poblanos Ranch in Albuquerque's North Valley.

Elinor Gregg Residence

Built in 1939 for Faith Meem's aunt, who had recently retired from a career with the Bureau of Indian Affairs in Washington, DC, the Gregg Residence wraps around a 16-ft-deep (5.6 m) portal oriented for solar gain and to capture views southwest of the Cerrillos Hills, Sandias, and La Tetilla.

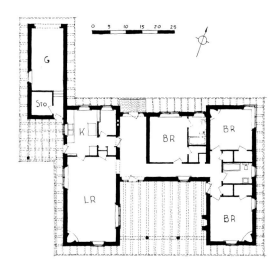

PROPOSED TERRACES
FOR "LA RESOLANA"

MEEM & McCORMICK, ARCHT'S.

PATIOS, TERRACES, AND GARDENS

As with many other aspects of Meem's designs, the relationship of his houses to nature and the outdoors was influenced by local Spanish traditions, Mexican and Spanish gardens, and recent reinterpretation of the Spanish tradition by other Sunbelt architects. In each of these locations, a temperate, arid climate favored the creation of outdoor rooms—tranquil oases of greenery and coursing water.

In the few full-courtyard houses Meem designed, the enclosed court is lined by portales. Frequently, he unfolded the wings of a house on two or three sides of a patio and completed the enclosure with masonry walls. When the site commanded landscape views, Meem created terraces sheltered in part by the house but with low retaining walls to leave the view open.

The transition from inside to out is gradual. Porches and solar portales provide rooms open on one side to the garden. Potted plants or long, narrow flowerbeds set between porch posts nevertheless direct people toward particular entrances into the garden. It helps that Meem's houses sit low to the ground rather than on raised foundations (as was the Anglo-American practice) so that porch flagstone floors flow easily down one or two short steps to flagstone terraces. The cracks between the terrace flagstones are often planted with a ground cover. As the cracks widen and flagstone walks finally reach like fingers out into the garden, the preponderance of brown over green gradually reverses. At the transition between different terrace levels, long narrow flowerbeds or potted plants again help compartmentalize space and direct people toward short flights of stairs.

"Proposed Terraces for La Resolana," Steadman Residence (1928). Hollenback Residence.

Conkey Residence.

Meem Residence.

Although plants were typically limited to pots and small beds in Spanish and Mexican gardens, Meem often added a small green lawn in deference to the suburban, pastoral expectations of clients transplanted from the East and Midwest. In these cases, a low stone curb or retaining wall makes a definite boundary between the lawn and an arid landscape of indigenous plants that can survive on the 14 in (35 cm) of annual precipitation at Santa Fe or the 8 in (20 cm) at Albuquerque.

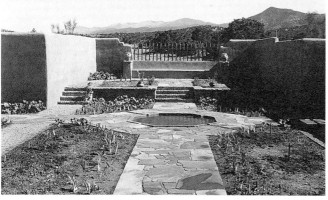

DESIGN · FOR · A · GARDEN · GATE ·
· TILNEY · RESIDENCE ·
SCALE · 1" = 1 Ft.   John Gaw Meem · Archt

In some of Meem's most secluded patios, octagonal, or star-shaped, fountains, covered in bright tiles kept glistening by running water, provide a dash of color when flowers are not in bloom. These typically sit at the center of symmetrical gardens where radial paths intersect. In houses with prominent views, a formal axis established in the house sometimes continues out through a symmetrical garden to its visual termination in a distant mountain peak. In more urban settings, where such views are not available, the undulating top of an adobe-brown garden wall becomes a surrogate for mesas and mountains.

Proctor Residence garden orients on Santa Fe Baldy. (Ansel Adams)

Garden gate mimics Sunmount, Conkey Residence. (Ansel Adams)

West garden, McCormick Residence

Garden gate, Tilney Residence (1929).

West garden, McCormick Residence.

opposite: South terrace, McCormick Residence

PART III
DESIGN IDIOMS

REFINING THE SPANISH-PUEBLO REVIVAL: THE CONKEY RESIDENCE, 1928

John Gaw Meem's first mature residential design, and one of his finest, was the 1928 Conkey Residence. His client, Mary Vilura Conkey, was born and raised in the far upstate New York town of Canton, where she graduated from St. Lawrence University. After attending Columbia University, she became a teacher of Latin and Greek in a private girls' school. In 1918, her health forced her to come west to Sunmount Sanitarium. When John Meem arrived at the sanitarium two years later, they formed a warm friendship that would last until her death in 1963.

Even after they recovered their health, Meem, Conkey, and other Sunmount patients continued to live in cottages on the sanitarium grounds and participate in its cultural life. So when Conkey turned her thoughts to building a residence of her own after ten years at the sanitarium, it was only natural to purchase a nearby hillside site from the sanitarium director, Dr. Mera, and ask Meem to undertake a design. Meem made a virtue of the site's steep slope when he created a richly modulated, ascending entry sequence, punctuated by architectural features and carefully framed landscape views.

Perspective from the southwest. (Gordon Street)

Plan.

opposite: Garden and back of long portal.

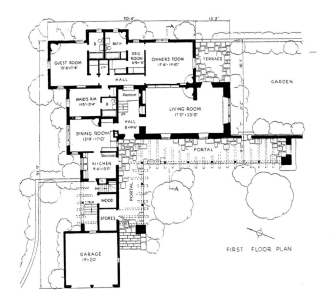

FIRST FLOOR PLAN

Diagram of entry path features. (George C. Pearl)

Original garage doors and long portal. (Ansel Adams)

Visitors approach the Conkey Residence by a winding gravel driveway, through scraggly piñon pine to a turnaround loop just below the house and the outstretched arms of its portales (see illustration on p. 25). The wood-grain texture of the Territorial Revival garage doors set in sloping adobe-colored walls announce a rustic vocabulary. First three steps, then a flagstone landing, then another eight steps flanked by a stepping buttress lead to a portal framed by a stout adobe pier. On reaching the porch landing, an antique door to the left reveals the inspiration for the garage doors, while the second arm of the portal with its carved corbel brackets opens to the right. Directly ahead, a provincial Greek Revival door topped by a triangular pediment provides a formal, visual goal. Pausing to wait after knocking on this door, a visitor might notice the delicate, lathe-turned porch balustrade or a shuttered, window-sized opening set in a solid adobe wall at the portal's end to the right. Once in the dark entry hall, one's eyes are drawn forward and up to the light from a hidden skylight ahead—the culmination of the entry sequence. The raised landing, a fragment of railing, and a hidden light source from above evoke the sanctuaries of New Mexico missions, which are similarly bathed with light from above.

Diagram of framed landscape views from living room and portales. (George C. Pearl)

Left of the entry hall, the dining room echoes the shape of the living room and its ceiling beams, mid-wall fireplace, and large, three-part window—but at a reduced scale. Since the dining room is cut a few feet into the earth, its windowsill is nearly level with the ground outside and offers an intimate close-up view of the gravelly hillside, the underside of piñon trees, and scattered tufts of dry grass and wild flowers.

The living room to the right measures 20 by 35 ft (6.1 by 10.7 m). Two-thirds of the way down the left-hand wall, a stepping paredcito projects 5 ft (1.5 m) into the room to create a right angle, which accommodates a traditional corner fireplace. The rhythm of the vigas and ornate corbels overhead unify this large, open room. But the fireplace simultaneously articulates the room into two unequal parts. A couch and a pair of easy chairs by the fireplace provide a setting for dinner party cocktails, while a chair or two pulled up to the window seat at the far end becomes the setting for afternoon tea among intimates.

The three-part living room window frames a view of Sunmount and begins the turn away from the ascending entry sequence, back out to the desert landscape. Exiting the front door, the L-shaped portal offers a vast panorama to the southwest of the Sandia Mountains, the Ortiz, the Cerrillos Hills, La Tetilla, and the southern flanks of the Jemez Mountains (now largely obscured by landscaping that has matured since the construction of the house). A visitor might walk to the end of the longer portal to study the carefully framed view of Sunmount to the south, before retreating along the entry axis toward a glimpse of the Jemez to the west. Hand-carved posts, beams, corbels, and shutters not only frame the views, but, when the sunlight rakes across their weathered wood grain, they also provide a textured, visceral analog close at hand for the play of light across the distant landscape.

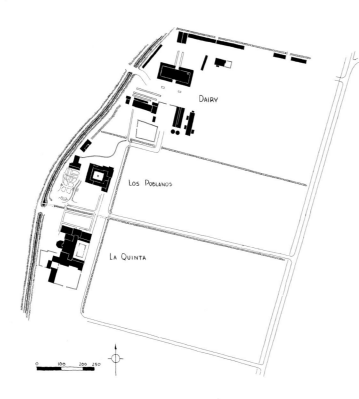

Los Poblanos Ranch site plan, based on 1947 aerial photo. (George C. Pearl)

opposite

Allée of cottonwoods on axis between Los Poblanos and La Quinta.

CREATING THE TERRITORIAL REVIVAL: LOS POBLANOS RANCH, 1932–35

Banker and land developer Albert Simms established Los Poblanos Ranch during the 1920s in the Rio Grande Valley just north of Albuquerque. During his term in the U.S. Congress at the end of the decade, he met Ruth Hanna McCormick, herself a congressional representative from Illinois, widow of Illinois senator Joseph McCormick, and the daughter of Ohio senator Marcus Hanna, who was a leading advisor to Republican presidents McKinley and Theodore Roosevelt. They married in 1932, after both lost their seats in a Democratic upswing. Ruth moved her Holstein breeding stock from Illinois to Los Poblanos to join Albert's Guernsey herd. With a combined herd of four hundred head, Albert joined with other producers to establish Albuquerque's Creamland Dairies.

After the marriage, Ruth initiated a collaboration with John Meem first to enlarge the existing adobe ranch house into a full courtyard house, which became known as Los Poblanos, and later to erect an even larger entertainment building christened La Quinta. Two of Meem's finest designs, they stand today along with dairy and service buildings amid extensive gardens on the remaining 26-acre core of the ranch.

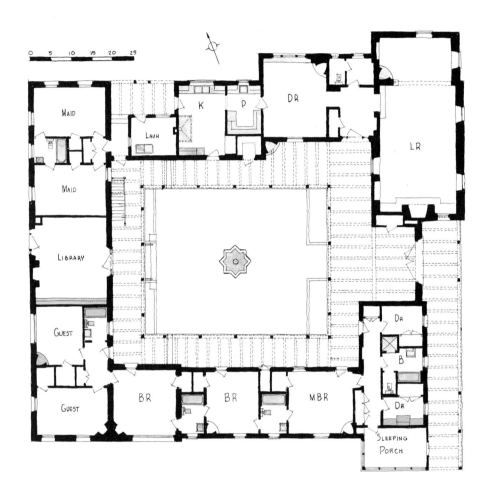

Los Poblanos

The original L-shaped, adobe ranch house (today the west side and first room on the south side of Los Poblanos) stood on a small rise at the western end of the property near a major irrigation canal, an acequia. Meem created a full courtyard house lined by a uniform portal that implies that the plan is symmetrical. However, he projected a sleeping porch on one side to provide better ventilation and a large living room to the other, which yielded an entry facade broader than the balance of the house behind.

Although the asymmetrical facade suggests informality, the heavy, double doors initiate a strong visual axis that continues across the patio and its star-shaped fountain to a formal door with side lights on the opposite side. Meem placed planting beds along the east and west sides of the patio, which channel movement into the patio along the entry axis. These beds also serve to reduce the rectangular patio to a square paved surface with the eight-pointed star fountain at its center. The glistening fountain tiles, along with the brick, squared flagstone and tile walks, provide color and texture throughout the seasons. In summer, terra-cotta pots bloom with flowers and fragrant herbs. Just inside the patio, the wider portal to the right pulls the visitor to another door with side lights and, to its left, a sitting area with outdoor fireplace.

Inside, the entry hall opens left, into a dining room seating eight, and right to the living room. A fireplace centered on the far wall draws attention first, but after descending the two steps into the room, one notices the informal alcove to the left with its own Spanish fireplace. The conventional groupings of rooms, which Meem often projected into separate wings of sprawling houses, are clustered here at the corners of the courtyard: the living room, dining room, and entry hall to the northeast; pantry, kitchen, laundry, and servants' rooms to the northwest; guest rooms to the southwest; and separate owners' suite to the southeast.

Dining room.

opposite
Living-room alcove fireplace.

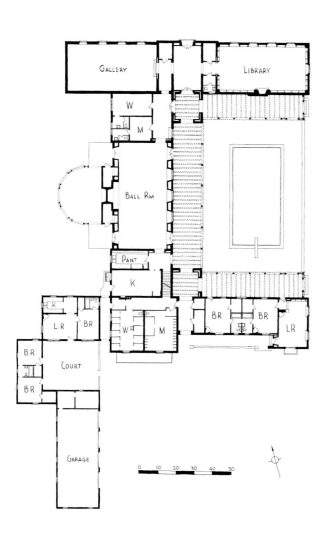

Perspective of La Quinta. (D. S. Morse)

La Quinta plan. (George C. Pearl)

opposite North facade.

La Quinta

In April 1934, John Meem was finishing the Colorado Springs Fine Arts Center and had just begun work on a new administration building for the University of New Mexico. However, on April 28, he drove from his Santa Fe office to Los Poblanos, where he and Ruth Simms devoted a day and a half to discussing her new project. By the end of his visit, they had decided on a one-story building just south of Los Poblanos facing east towards the Sandias. A new formal driveway would approach through an allée of trees toward a lawn between the two buildings, turn left in front of La Quinta, and left again on its way back to the street. La Quinta's centerpiece would be a ballroom capable of seating two hundred for concerts, and boasting a fine dance floor and elaborate carved ceiling. There would also be coat- and powder rooms, a large caterer's pantry, and an apartment, which her son, John McCormick, would occupy during the summer. Meem and Simms envisioned an L-shaped building with walls completing an enclosure around a swimming pool.

Later, as Simms's conception of La Quinta matured into a community center for Albuquerque, a library and art gallery were added to the program. With these additional components, Meem was able to develop a symmetrical H-shape plan with the ballroom in the middle linking the library and gallery wing on the north and the apartment, service and servants wing on the south.

Meem had initiated the development of the Territorial Revival style in the Los Poblanos ranch house. Now, in response to Ruth Simms's desire for a formal, quasi-public building with "no Indian motive," he further developed the classicism inherent in the provincial Greek Revival adobe buildings of New Mexico's Territorial period. Here (and in his contemporaneous FERA Building in Santa Fe), Meem settled on a Territorial Revival palette of light stucco walls, brick cornices, flat roofs, and white classical trim (see illustrations on pp. 74). This clas-

sical styling reinforced La Quinta's symmetry of plan and massing with its north and south wings flanking human-scaled porticos that lead to the taller cross portico and its five tall ballroom windows. To give the open ends of his entry porticos a strong termination and visual substance to the semi-octagonal west pavilion, Meem placed lattice between paired posts—a detail he had observed in the 1860s Baca House in Upper Las Vegas.

Ballroom. (Laura Gilpin)

   The size and grandeur of La Quinta was such, however, that Meem found himself looking beyond local historic precedents. The ballroom, for instance, was to be appreciably larger than the typical New Mexican sala, so Meem delved into Byrn and Stapley's 1920 monograph, *Decorated Wooden Ceilings in Spain*, which illustrated ceilings with large transverse beams topped by heavy exposed joists. But rather than applying painted decorations, as was the custom in Spain, Meem specified that the light California sugar pine be sanded, wire brushed, and carved with New Mexican decorative motifs: a Franciscan cord molding around the perimeter, geometricized Pueblo rain clouds on the underside of the beams, and a herringbone pattern in the decking.

Other books on Spanish and Mexican interiors in Meem's office library suggested heavy wooden shutters for the ballroom's large windows and doors. For the library, he similarly adapted American Colonial and Territorial-style moldings and paneling details, although in the art gallery interior he adopted a more restrained modernistic setting of cork flooring, plastered walls, simple cove moldings, and recessed lighting fixtures. Meem established a conventional hierarchy of floor materials: hard surfaces in high-traffic areas (flagstone under the entry portales; terra-cotta tile under the taller, western portal; bricks where the portales cross; and terra-cotta tiles with glazed tile accents in the entry halls) and a wooden parquet floor in the ballroom.

Befitting her conception of La Quinta as a quasi-public community arts center, Ruth Simms commissioned carved beams and doors reputedly from the Santa Fe wood block print master, Gustave Baumann. Meem allocated a number of blank panels and walls for murals as he did for major public buildings, and Simms subsequently commissioned the young Peter Hurd to fresco a mural of San Ysidro, the patron saint of farmers. The five panels painted by Harry Miller over the ballroom doors and windows portray a local pastoral history of sheepherding, irrigated farming, and, in the center panel, the Simms' own dairy barn and herds—albeit with low hills behind, rather than the tall Rio Grande cottonwoods that actually lined their property.

In 1938, just as the artists were finishing their work, Ruth's son, John McCormick, died in a climbing accident in the Sandia Mountains, and she entered a period of mourning. In 1940, she served as national co-chair for Thomas E. Dewey's campaign for president and, in April, hosted a rally with Dewey and three hundred Republican stalwarts in attendance at La Quinta. Then in 1944, Ruth Hanna McCormick Simms died unexpectedly at the age of 64, and La Quinta never matured into the envisioned community art center. Only in the late 1990s was it used regularly for receptions and group retreats as part of Armin and Penny Rembe's Los Poblanos Inn.

above
One of five murals by Harry Miller.

Portal ceiling.

below
Images of San Ysidro, patron of farmers, including mural by Peter Hurd.

opposite
Doors reputedly carved by Gustave Baumann.

SEEKING A CONTEMPORARY SOUTHWEST STYLE: THE MEEM RESIDENCE, 1937

Whenever the opportunity presented itself, John Gaw Meem incorporated existing buildings into his designs for new houses—never to better effect than in his own house. Soon after their marriage in 1933, Faith and John Meem purchased the Nagel farm southeast of Santa Fe, just across an arroyo from Sunmount Sanitarium. The three existing buildings conformed to the Hispanic vernacular in their flat-roofed stone and adobe construction and long narrow forms with multiple exterior doors. Located on a southwest-facing slope, the three buildings formed a U-shaped courtyard. The use of buildings to define plazas, courtyards, and terraces—to protect the north from winter winds and open on the south or southeast to the morning sun—is a local climatic adaptation practiced over the past thousand years by Anasazi, Pueblo, Hispanic, and Anglo builders.

The Meems first added portales to link the north and west buildings and converted the remaining building on the east into a garage. But they also wisely decided to live in this compound for a time—to observe daily and seasonal patterns and to find what they liked and disliked about the existing arrangements—before making plans for major additions. Their most important discovery came when Meem went up to fix a leaking roof over the garage and noticed that the landscape views were substantially better there than in the courtyard below.

To capture these views, he decided—undoubtedly in even closer consultation with his architect wife than was already their practice—to replace the garage with a large new structure.

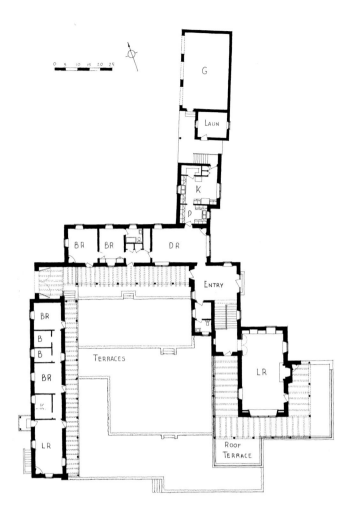

Meem reversed normal Anglo-American spatial patterns when he placed the bedrooms below, and a living room with rooftop terraces above. This arrangement, however, paralleled what he had observed at Acoma Pueblo, to which he had dispatched a HABS documentation crew in 1935. There, dwelling rooms on the second and third levels open directly onto rooftop terraces used for socializing and viewing dances and equipped with outdoor fireplaces and ovens for cooking.

His second major design decision was to relocate the driveway, which approached the house in a direct line to the garage. He shifted the entrance to the drive further southeast on Old Santa Fe Trail, so that it might climb a small rise to an overview of the house, then wind gently to a new parking court on the west, where an original building would screen the new two-story addition from view. This elegantly picturesque entry sequence continues with a glimpse of Sunmount over the top of a covered zaguan entry (characterized by heavy wooden double doors), which Meem placed at the knuckle between the original western and northern buildings. Passing through the zaguan, views open to the right down a descending portal to a guest apartment, ahead and right to the cascading garden and new two-story wing beyond, and straight ahead, on axis, to a formal Territorial-style doorway.

Meem Residence plan. (George C. Pearl)

In the ample entry hall, a large door with side lights directly opposite the main door offers a glimpse outside to a flower garden, while diagonally to the right a split stair leads down to the private family quarters and also up to a landing. Directly ahead at the top of the stairs, a door opens to roof terraces, which look back down on the entry portal and courtyard garden. Further along the terrace, views open to the south and west to the Sandia and Jemez Mountains and, proceeding around to the left, a secluded nook with an outdoor fireplace and a close view of Sunmount.

Alternately, at the stair landing, one turns left into a large living room with windows in each of its four walls. At the far end, a comfortable window seat provides a setting for afternoon teas or evening cocktails. At the middle of the long wall opposite, a large fireplace surrounded by a boldly molded frame forms a backdrop for informal remarks made, over the years, at Meem office Christmas parties and meetings of the Chili Club, the local chapter of the American Institute of Architects, and other civic groups, as well as conference and wedding receptions.

Living room (about 1940).

(Ernest Knee)

Hallway of lower bedroom wing, looking toward a folk Territorial door and stairs to the entry hall. (Ernest Knee)

The design of the house also reflects Meem's growing attempts throughout the 1930s to reconcile the regional tradition he so valued with Modernist theory and design. He considered the use of adobe for the new construction—he even stockpiled adobes on site—but ultimately decided on the use of stone from the nearby arroyo set in concrete mortar as the Nagels had for the earlier buildings. This satisfied the Modernist requirement that materials be used honestly, which adobe-colored cement stucco over adobe or hollow clay tile would have violated. (Stone faces adobe walls in the old portions and hollow tile in the new portions of the house.) The tree-trunk porch posts and simple round and square ceiling beams, with not a single carved corbel bracket, likewise acceded to the Modernist prohibition of ornament. Even the Territorial-style door and window trim evoked a classical precision consonant with Modernist rationality. The richly textured stone walls, flagstone and brick floors, and natural wood ceilings, along with the modular masonry masses and the garden courtyard and rooftop terraces, nevertheless, all build on strong regional traditions.

ACKNOWLEDGMENTS

In 1996, Nancy Meem Wirth, Beverly Spears, George O'Bryan, Peter Wirth, Doug McDowell, and Nancy Melin initiated an informal group to visit and study houses designed by John Gaw Meem. They invited Chris Wilson to join their group and, in time, encouraged us to undertake this book. We are indebted to them for initiating this project, conducting preliminary research, and helping gain access to Meem-designed houses.

The arrival at one's front door at the crack of dawn of a photographer with two or three assistants and extensive equipment, along with a writer with notebook in hand, can be somewhat unsettling. We greatly appreciate the hospitality of the owners and residents of Meem houses who graciously opened their doors to us: Flora Atherton, Mr. and Mrs. Stephen Bershad, Gary Bobolsky, Laura Carpenter, Ann Simms Clark, Edward Cook, Mary Jean Cook, John Crichton, K. K. Dendahl, Eileen Dodge, Perry Foster, Jay Grabb, Dan Haft, Steve Husbands, Dan Kelly Jr., Rachel Kelly, Jean Link, Orville Link, Dusty Loo, Jeannie Lyrus, Robin McKinney Martin, Meade Martin, Dr. and Mrs. David Ottenmeyer, Armin Rembe, Penny Rembe, Carol Romero Wirth, Douglas Schwartz, Nita Schwartz, Katina Simmons, Robert Walker, Victoria Walker, John Wirth, Nicholas Wirth, Nancy Wirth, and Peter Wirth.

—CHRIS WILSON AND ROBERT RECK

In 1980, Bainbridge Bunting asked me to assist him with the photography for a book on John Gaw Meem's architecture. Working on this current book about Meem's life and residential design has caused me to reflect on my gratitude to Bainbridge. It was his excitement and contagious enthusiasm for the built environment that was the genesis of my career in architectural photography, a career now spanning more than twenty years. Working on *Facing Southwest* with Chris Wilson has not only been a reconnection with the beginnings of my career, but a professionally and personally rewarding partnership. The discussions with Chris were invaluable as I sought to capture Meem's aesthetic expressions in photographic terms.

My unending appreciation and thanks to my longtime associate and studio manager, Mary Elkins, who has spent much of the last twenty years working with me, has provided patience, support, and counsel, and has contributed immeasurably to my work. Matt Gray and Sarah Dawson also deserve thanks for their able assistance during long hours shooting on location.

—ROBERT RECK

John Gaw Meem's career as a preservationist, civic leader, and architect of public buildings figures prominently in my earlier book, *The Myth of Santa Fe: Creating a Modern Regional Tradition.* His residences, however, receive only this brief (and, as it turns out, fairly accurate) summary comment in an endnote: "Meem houses have rambling asymmetric plans that hug the ground and open to outdoor living spaces, much like the West Coast houses of Wright, Neutra, Harris and Wurster. Not only did Meem wrap his houses around gardens and porches, but he often widened his portales into outdoor rooms with fireplaces and built-in benches, and oriented to landscape views or direct sunlight." Enlarging that comment into this book has been a distinct pleasure, enhanced by the many people who offered assistance, advice, and encouragement. In addition to those already mentioned, my appreciation and warm regards goes to the following individuals.

Throughout this project—by welcoming me into her home, agreeing to be interviewed at length, providing access to family photographs, helping us gain access to other houses, and carefully reviewing the manuscript—Nancy Meem Wirth was unstinting in her support and encouragement. George Clayton Pearl, a distinguished architect in the New Mexican tradition, not only served as my primary sounding board and made invaluable comments on drafts of the manuscript, he also generously volunteered to produce the supplemental plans and diagrams that add so much to this publication. I also owe a particular debt of gratitude to Anne Boynton, David Margolin, Beverly Spears, and John Wirth for their close readings of the manuscript. Thomas Hubka, Victor Johnson, Claudia Smith, and Anne Tyler provided timely advice and assistance. In interviews with me, Katrina Barnes, Anne Simms Clark, Edward T. Hall, Van Dorn Hooker, Albert Simms, Barbara Simms, Robert Stamm, and John Wirth offered invaluable personal insights on Meem.

Among those who assisted in the securing of illustrations and reproduction permissions are Arthur Olivas and Dick Rudisill, Photo Archives, History Museum, Museum of New Mexico, Santa Fe; Sandra Jaramillo and José Villegas, Santa Fe State Records Center and Archives, Santa Fe; Courtney DeAngelis, Amon Carter Museum, Ft. Worth, Texas; Carolyn Cooper, Ansel Adams Publishing Trust, Mill Valley, California; and Gene Kuntz, Santa Fe Editions Gallery. Jan Barnhart, Office of Development and Public Affairs, General Libraries; and Marilyn Fletcher, Kathlene Ferris, Stella De Sa Rego, Nancy Brown, and Ann Massmann, Center for Southwest Research, Zimmerman Library, at the University of New Mexico, where the Meem office archives are located, deserve a special thanks for their long, patient assistance.

My final, and most heartfelt, thanks are for my parents Martin and Joanne Wilson, my wife, Kathryn Williams, and our son, Luc Wilson, whose love and support mean the world to me.

—CHRIS WILSON

NOTES

PART I: FACING SOUTHWEST

1. John Gaw Meem (JGM), notes of conference with Mr. and Mrs. Ferdinand Koch, August 1928, job 99, Meem Papers, John Gaw Meem Archives of Southwestern Architecture, Zimmerman Library, University of New Mexico, Albuquerque (MC).

2. Like his uncle James Meem's Underpinning and Foundation Company, or his architectural mentors, Fisher & Fisher, indeed like any professional firm of the era, John Gaw Meem's office kept thorough, well-organized files on all of its projects, as well as Meem's civic activities. These notes of client conferences, correspondence with clients, builders and suppliers, internal office memos, design sketches, construction drawings, and photographs are housed in the Meem Papers at the University of New Mexico, Albuquerque (MC). These are organized by the original office job numbers, which are referenced in notes below. I also visited approximately twenty houses designed by Meem and conducted interviews with Lillian Armit, November 26, 1984; Katrina Barnes (daughter of Ruth Hanna McCormick Simms), November 29, 1997; Dr. F. Martin Brown, November 27, 1984; Anne Simms Clark, December 1, 1997; Edward T. Hall, March 14, 1997; Van Dorn Hooker, December 5, 1997; Faith Bemis Meem, December 13, 1984; Dr. Albert and Barbara Simms, December 4, 1997; Robert Stamm, December 3, 1997; Nancy Meem Wirth, November 14, and 28, 1997 and June 10, 1998; John Wirth, December, 1997; Mrs. Walter Wood (Olive Burke), November 27, 1984.

3. On the background of the Meem and Krischke families see Bainbridge Bunting, *John Gaw Meem: Southwest Architect* (Albuquerque: University of New Mexico Press, 1983), 3; Arthur L. De- Volder, "John Gaw Meem, F.A.I.A.: An Appreciation," *New Mexico Historical Review*, July 1979, 209–225; John C. McNary, "John Gaw Meem: His Style Development and Residential Architecture Between 1924 and 1940," M.A. thesis, University of New Mexico, 1977, 3.

4. Bunting, 3; DeVolder, 209; McNary, 3; B. M. Read, "John Gaw Meem '14," *Virginia Military Institute Alumni Review*, Fall 1978, 2.

5. Bunting, 3–5; DeVolder, 209–210; McNary, 3–5.

6. Bunting, 4–9; Chris Wilson, *The Myth of Santa Fe: Creating a Modern Regional Tradition* (Albuquerque: University of New Mexico Press, 1997), especially chapter 4.

7. Bunting, 9–12; DeVolder, 210–211; McNary, 7–8; Wayne Mauzy, "Sunmount Vital Force in City Life," *Santa Fe New Mexican*, Centennial-Fiesta Edition, 1949, Section 7, 2.

8. Bunting, 8; DeVolder, 212–213; Architects' Small House Service, Mountain Division, *How to Plan, Finance, and Build Your Home* (Denver: Author, 1922); Thomas J. Noel and Barbara S. Norgren, *Denver: The City Beautiful* (Denver: Denver Historical Society, 1987), 198–200, 203–204.

9. Bunting, 12–14; DeVolder, 212; McNary, 9.

10. John Harbeson and Beaux-Arts Institute of America, *The Study of Architectural Design* (New York: Pencil Points Press, 1927); Gwendolyn Wright and Janet Parks, eds., *The History of History in American Schools of Architecture*, 1865–1975 (New York: Princeton Architectural Press, 1990), 13–72; Elisabeth Blair McDougall, ed., *The Architectural Historian in America* (Washington DC: National Gallery of Art, 1990), 61–76.

11. John Gaw Meem, "An Entrance to a Museum," *American Architect*, October 1923, 19.

12. Carl D. Sheppard, *Creator of the Santa Fe Style: Isaac Hamilton Rapp* (Albuquerque: University of New Mexico Press, 1988). Meem's first completed design, a portal addition for Mrs. Knox Taylor, is dated January 1925.

13. JGM to Mamie Meadors, January 22, 1927, job 16, MC; JGM to Misses Hownells, October 14, 1930, job 136, MC: See job correspondence files for houses designed for Mary Austin (3), Albert and Ruth Hanna McCormick Simms (191, 237), Mary Vilura Conkey (92), Amelia Hollenback (148), Mamie Meadors (16), Eleanor Brownell and Alice Howland (136, 286).

14. JGM to Dr. and Mrs. F. I. Proctor, January 18, 1929, and F. I. Proctor to JGM, January 8, 1929, job 109, MC.

15. Bunting, 37–57, 73–106, 157; DeVolder, 216; "Indian Museum in New Mexico Picks Architect," *New York Herald*, January 12, 1930.

16. Wilson, *Myth*, 281; "The Carlos Vierra House," *Bulletin of the Historic Santa Fe Association*, January 1979; Chamber of Commerce House Design Competition file, Photo Archives, History Library, Museum of New Mexico, Santa Fe.

17. Bunting, 23–26, 47–49, 128–142; NcNary, 67, 72–73, 79–81, 135, 153–157. See also drawings, photos, and correspondence files for houses designed for Henry Galt (0), Mrs. Ashley Pond (3), Meadors-Staples-Anthony (16), Emory Steadman (18), Tom R. Wyles (19), and Dr. J. R. Rolls (45), MC.

18. JGM to Emory A. Steadman, October 7, 1925, job 18-a, MC; Laboratory of Anthropology Director's Residence, bid specifications, job 138a, MC.

19. JGM to Emory A. Steadman, October 7, 1925, job 18, MC; Laboratory of Anthropology Director's Residence, bid specifications, job 138a, MC.

20. Harbeson, *Study of Architectural Design*, quotation, 19. Mark Alan Hewitt, *The Architect and the American Country House, 1890–1940* (New Haven: Yale University Library, 1990), 52–53, 109; Richard Longstreth, "Academic Eclecticism in American Architecture," *Winterthur Portfolio*, September 1983, 56–82.

21. Mission Preservation: Bunting, 9–10, 42–46; DeVolder, 212–213; McNary, 11–15; Wilson, *Myth*, 238–244; Beatrice Chauvenet, *John Gaw Meem: Pioneer in Historic Preservation* (Santa Fe: Museum of New Mexico Press, 1985).

Although it was a common practice in the late nineteenth and early twentieth centuries, the removal of architectural details from historic buildings for reuse in new buildings is strongly opposed today by most historic preservationists.

22. Carlos Vierra, "Carlos Vierra Photograph Albums from the John Gaw Meem Archives of Southwestern Architecture" (Albuquerque, NM: Center for Southwest Research); Lippincott file, MC; notebooks of photographic copies of HABS drawings completed under the direction of John Meem from January 15, 1934 to September 26, 1940, located in Center for Southwest Research, UNM, MC [original drawings at Library of Congress].

23. On the Romantic tradition in architecture: Vincent Scully Jr., *The Shingle Style and the Stick Style: Architectural Theory and Designs from Richardson to the Origins of Wright* (New Haven: Yale University Press, 1955). The Ruskin and Downing books remain in Meem's private library in the Meem-Wirth Residence, Santa Fe.

24. John Gaw Meem, "Monuments of New Mexico," type script of talk delivered at American Institute of Architects annual conference, San Antonio, Texas, 1931, box 3, folder 24, MC, 4.

25. Meem, "Monuments," 5.

26. Rexford Newcomb, *The Spanish House for America* (Philadelphia: Lippincott, 1927); Scully, *Shingle Style*; *Wallace Neff, 1895–1982: The Romance of Regional Architecture* (San Marino, California: The Huntington Library, 1989); Donald W. Curl, *Minzer's Florida: American Resort Architecture* (Cambridge, MA: MIT Press, 1984).

27. Hewitt, 90, 113, 211, 221; R. W. Sexton, *Spanish Influence on American Architecture and Decoration* (New York: Brentanos, 1927), 14.

28. Newcomb, *The Spanish Home*; Rexford Newcomb, *Spanish-Colonial Architecture in the United States* (1937, rpt. New York: Dover, 1990).

29. Bunting, 130–133. Reconstruction of Meem's design procedures based on the extensive project files in MC.

30. JGM to Mrs. Albert Simms, October 9, 1934, job 237, MC.

31. JGM to Dr. Lothrop, undated, job 497, MC; JGM to Eleanor Brownell, October 5, 1937, job 286, MC.

32. Eastern and California estate names culled from Hewitt,

The Architect, and Clive Aslet, *The American Country House* (New Haven: Yale University Press, 1990). Named Meem houses: La Resolana (E. Steadman Residence, 18), Las Acequias (Cyrus McCormick Residence, 130), Los Piñones (Mary V. Conkey Residence, 92), Los Poblanos (Albert and Ruth Simms Residence, 191), and La Quinta (Ruth and Albert Simms' recreation building, 237).

33. JGM to Alice Howland, 1940, job 286, MC.

34. Cyrus McCormick Jr. to John D. Rockefeller Jr., January 6, 1930, MC, file 130.

35. On the rise of the American business oligarchy and country houses see: Hewett, especially, x–xi, 10–15.

36. Hewitt, 13, 89; MC, files for Hollenback Residence (148), McCormick Residence (130), Los Alamos Ranch School (196), Fountain Valley School (146), and Sandia Girls School (255).

37. JGM to Cyrus McCormick Jr., August 26, 1929, job 130, MC; Bunting, 46–48.

38. Bunting, 29–31; McCormick Residence, job 130, MC.

39. Hollenback to JGM, October 28, 1930, job 148, MC; Bunting, 138–142; Wilson, *Myth*, 246.

40. JGM to Frank Chase, April 10, 1930, job 133, MC.

41. Frank Chase to JGM: October 16, 1930; November 14, 1930; January 14, 1931; and additional correspondence, job 133, MC; "Building for the Journal Company, Milwaukee, Frank D. Chase Inc., Engineers and Architects," *American Architect*, November 20, 1925, 435–439; "Campana Factory, Batavia, Illinois, Frank D. Chase, and Childs and Smith Associated Architects and Engineers," *Architectural Record*, December 1930, 500–502.

42. Frank Chase to JGM, September 4, 1931, and JGM to Chase, September 9, 1931, job 131, MC.

43. Frank Chase to JGM, March 18, 1937, and JGM to Chase, March 24, 1937, job 131, MC.

44. Meem, "Monuments of New Mexico."

45. Meem quoted in Chris Wilson, "A Unique Opportunity: John Gaw Meem and the Colorado Springs Fine Arts Center," in Josie D. Kerstetter ed., *Colorado Springs Fine Arts Center: A History and Selections from the Permanent Collections* (Colorado Springs: Colorado Springs Fine Arts Center, 1986), 31.

46. F. R. S. Yorke, *The Modern House* (London: The Architectural Press, 1934), copy inscribed to Meem in John Gaw Meem Southwestern Architecture Collection, Zimmerman Library, University of New Mexico, Albuquerque. Faith Bemis Meem biography: McNary, 24; DeVolder, 219; Bob Quick, "Faith Meem, Active to the End, Dies at Home," *Santa Fe New Mexican*, March 24, 1989.

47. Bunting, 23–26; Wilson, *Myth*, 277–281; John Gaw Meem, "Old Forms for New Buildings," *American Architect*, November 1934, 10–21.

48. Meem, "Old Forms for New Buildings."

49. Sandra D'Emilio, Suzan Campbell, and John Kessel, *Spirit and Vision: Images of Ranchos de Taos Church* (Santa Fe: Museum of New Mexico Press, 1987).

50. Bunting 145–154; Wilson, "A Unique Opportunity."

51. Memo of conference with Mr. and Mrs. Tilney, Jan. 30, 1929, job 117, MC. See also drawings for Ashley Pond (3), and Conkey Residences (92), MC.

52. Bunting, 105–166; McNary, 101–103. See also drawings, photographs, and correspondence files for houses designed for Isabel Eccles (175), Ruth and Albert Simms (Los Poblanos, 191), James McLane (195), MC.

53. Ruth Hanna McCormick Simms to JGM, undated [about September 25, 1934], job 237, MC. See also: Wilson, *Myth*, 281–286, and MC files for the FERA Building (242) and John Simms Residence (245).

54. JGM to Eleanor Brownell, December 6, 1937, job 286, MC; JGM to Regional Director, National Park Service, November 23, 1939 [priorities for historic buildings to measure], HABS files, MC. See also files for the Nordhaus (253) and Clendenin Residences (312), MC.

55. Bunting, 142–147; drawings and photos of houses designed for Elinor Gregg and Ruth Heflin, MC, files 323, 336.

56. Van Dorn Hooker, *Only in New Mexico: An Architectural History of the University of New Mexico, 1889–1989* (Albuquerque: UNM Press, 2000), 100.

57. JGM to Dr. and Mrs. (Ted and Joan) Mathews, August 31, 1940, in Nancy Meem Wirth, ed., *Box 628: Recollections and Letters, 1940–1944* (Atherton, CA: publisher unknown, 1990), 153–156 [copy available at MC].

58. Bunting, 28–29, 57–71; reapplication for military service, World War II file, MC.

59. JGM, "The Negro Problem in America," 1943 talk, in Nancy

Meem Wirth, ed., *Chili Club Papers by John Gaw Meem, 1939–1976,* 1994, 43–52, MC.

60. JGM, "The Negro Problem in America," in *Chili Club Papers.*

61. Santa Fe Builders Supply Company (Sanbusco), job 404, MC.

62. Ford-Libby-Owens correspondence, plans, and select perspectives, job 460, MC; Mason Simon, *Your Solar Home* (New York: Simon & Schuster, 1947), 110–111.

63. JGM, "Memorandum of Conference with Dr. and Mrs. W. R. Lovelace II," August 16, 1946, job 474, MC.

64. Meem notes of a "Conference with Mr. and Mrs. L. G. Phillips," September 1945, job 459, MC.

65. Mrs. Violet Phillips to JGM, October 23, 1946, and JGM to Mrs. Phillips, November 7, 1946, job 459, MC.

66. Jay Furey Muntz, "Bubbles for Defence," in *Wallace Neff.* Houses in Meem's extended eave, contemporary idiom were designed in 1945–47 for John Baker (482), Dr. Sidney Auerbach (518), Dr. Albert Lothrop (497), Christine Hughs (530), J. R. Cole (509), John Walter (520), and Dr. and Mrs. Bartlett T. Dewey (434).

67. Bunting, 86–106; DeVolder, 216.

68. On use of color: Frank Chase to JGM, November 26, 1929, job 133, MC; JGM, "Color Schedule for R. J. Nordhaus Residence," July 17, 1937, job 253, MC; Alice Howland to JGM, November 10, 1940, and JGM to Alice Howland, November 18, 1940, job 286, MC; "Paint Schedule—Ruth Heflin's House," job 336, MC; "Formulas for Mixing Tecolite Colors," and Faber Birren, "Functional Color and the Architect," in *Color: Technical Reference Guide No. 4* (Washington DC: American Institute of Architects, 1949), Color Pamphlets, General Information file, MC.

69. Mary Lovelace to JGM, November 4, 1947, job 474, MC. See also files for Everett Jones (590), McHarg Davenport (651), and James Rogers (662) Residences, MC.

70. House designs incorporating bay windows include those for Mr. and Mrs. Allen W. Hinkel (568), Everett Jones (590), and McHarg Davenport (651), MC.

71. Bunting, 20–21; DeVolder, 221–223; Wilson, *Myth,* 259–262, 287–291.

PART II: DESIGN PATTERNS

Parts II and III are based on an analysis of correspondence, working drawings, and photographs for numerous houses in MC-UNM. Particularly extensive documentation exists for houses designed for Proctor (file #109), McCormick/Las Acequias (130), Chase (133), Brownell-Howland I (136), Hollenback (148), Simms/Los Poblanos (191), Simms/La Quinta (233), and Brownell-Howland II (286). Only specific quoted documents and supplemental published sources are cited here.

Floor Plans
Meem's house designs parallel the discussions of two books in his library: Newcomb, *Spanish House,* chapter 2; R. W. Sexton, *Spanish Influence on American Architecture and Decoration* (New York: Brentanos, 1927), chapter 1.

Picturesque and Classical Composition
Quotations: JGM to Frank Chase, January 4, 1930, MC-UNM, file 133; Wilson, "A Unique Opportunity," 32; Kelbaugh, *Common Place,* 79; John Gaw Meem, "Monuments of New Mexico." See also Newcomb, *Spanish House,* 14, 20–24, 42, 45; Alexander, *Pattern Language,* patterns 110, 116.

Entry Paths
Quote: Newcomb, *Spanish House,* 30. Stefanos Polyzoides, Roger Sherwood, and James Tice, *Courtyard Housing in Los Angeles* (1982, rpt. New York: Princeton Architectural Press, 1992), discusses the interrelation of Hollywood and the Spanish Revival.

Salas and Living Rooms
See also Alexander, *Pattern Language,* patterns 129, 191, 196.
Alcoves and Window Seats
Quote: JGM, "Memo, Frank D. Chase Residence," June 4, 1929, MC, file 133. See also Alexander, pattern 202.

Fireplaces
Quote: JGM to Frank Chase, March 20, 1931, job 133, MC. See also Newcomb, *Spanish House,* chapter 13; Alexander, pattern 202.

Ceilings and Floors
Quotes: JGM to Summit Pressed Brick and Tile Company, Pueblo, CO, November 9, 1929, MC, file 92; JGM to Cyrus McCormick Jr., August 26, 1929, job 130, MC. See also: Newcomb, *Spanish House*, chapter 12; Alexander, patterns 190, 232.

Doors
Newcomb, *Spanish House*, chapter 6.

Built-ins
Newcomb, *Spanish House*, 105; Alexander, patterns 197, 198.

Solar Portales and Living Porches
Alexander, patterns 163, 175; Simon, *Your Solar*.

Patios, Terraces, and Gardens
Meem's designs of patios and terraces parallel the discussions of three books in his library: Newcomb, *Spanish House*, chapter 15; Mildred and Arthur Bryn, *Spanish Gardens and Patios* (Philadelphia: Lippincott, 1924); Richard S. Requa, *Old World Inspiration for American Architects* (Denver: Monolith Portland Midwest Company, 1929). See also Alexander, patterns 105, 106, 168.

PART III: DESIGN IDIOMS

The Conkey Residence
"Mary V. Conkey, Long Time SF Resident, Dies," *Daily New Mexican*, September 17, 1963, 7; and correspondence, working drawings, and photographs for Mary Vilura Conkey Residence, job 92, MC.

Los Poblanos
Bunting, *John Gaw Meem*, 106–113; "Los Poblanos Ranch," *Country Life in America*, November 1938, 80–85; "[Ruth Hanna McCormick] Simms Rites To Be Thursday," *Santa Fe New Mexican*, January 2, 1945, 6; "[Albert G.] Simms Rites Thursday in Duke City," *Santa Fe New Mexican*, December 30, 1964, 2; Kathryn Sargent and Mary Davis, *Shining River, Precious Land:*

An Oral History of Albuquerque's North Valley (Albuquerque: Albuquerque Museum, 1986), 155–164; Robert Metzger, ed., *My Land is the Southwest: Peter Hurd Letters and Journals* (College Station: Texas A&M Press, 1983); Joanne Seale Lawson, "Remarkable Foundations: Rose Isabel Greely, Landscape Architect," *Washington History*, Spring/Summer 1998, 67–68. The brief quotation and the program for La Quinta are contained in JGM, "Memorandum of Conversation with Mrs. Albert G. Simms," April 28, 1934. Inspirations for ballroom ceiling design: Arthur Byne and Mildred Stapley, *Decorated Wooden Ceilings in Spain* (New York: Putnam, 1920), plates II, IV. Inspiration for ballroom shutters: Byne and Stapley, *Spanish Interiors and Furniture* (New York: William Helburn, 1928), plates 47, 48, 153.

Ruth Simms also engaged landscape architect Rose Greely (a classmate of Faith Meem at the Cambridge School of Architecture and Landscape Architecture), who had designed a garden for her Washington residence, to design gardens to the south and west of Los Poblanos. Although Greely established a cross-axial plan in accordance with Beaux-Arts principles, these gardens wrap the bedroom wings and therefore have no strong architectural axis with which to link. The formal flower gardens on the west were most fully realized, including pebble-embedded concrete walkways by Tom Perea and "Pop" Schaefer, who is remembered today for his folk gardens at the Schaefer Hotel in Mountainair, New Mexico.

The Meem Residence
Bunting, 142–145.

BIBLIOGRAPHY

Alexander, Christopher, Sara Isikawa, and Murray Silverstein. *A Pattern Language*. New York: Oxford University Press, 1977.

Aslet, Clive. *The American Country House*. New Haven: Yale University Press, 1990.

Baca, Elmo. *Santa Fe Design*. Lincolnwood, IL: Publications International, 1990.

Belloli, Andres P. A., ed. *Wallace Neff, 1895–1982: The Romance of Regional Architecture*. San Marino, CA: The Huntington Library, 1989.

Bryn, Mildred, and Arthur Bryn. *Spanish Gardens and Patios*. Philadelphia: Lippincott, 1924.

Bunting, Bainbridge. *Early Architecture of New Mexico*. Albuquerque: University of New Mexico Press, 1976.

———. *John Gaw Meem: Southwest Architect*. Albuquerque: University of New Mexico Press, 1983.

———. *Taos Adobes: Spanish Colonial and Territorial Architecture of the Taos Valley*. Santa Fe: Museum of New Mexico Press, 1964.

Chauvenet, Beatrice. *John Gaw Meem: Pioneer in Historic Preservation*. Santa Fe: Museum of New Mexico Press, 1985.

Congress for the New Urbanism. *Charter for the New Urbanism*. New York: McGraw-Hill, 1999.

Curl, Donald W. *Minzer's Florida: American Resort Architecture*. Cambridge, MA: MIT Press, 1984.

Davis, Howard. *The Culture of Building*. New York: Oxford University Press, 1999.

D'Emilio, Sandra, Suzan Campbell, and John Kessell. *Spirit and Vision: Images of Ranchos de Taos Church*. Santa Fe: Museum of New Mexico Press, 1987.

Dennis, Landt, and Lisl Dennis. *Behind Adobe Walls: The Hidden Homes and Gardens of Santa Fe and Taos*. San Francisco: Chronicle Books, 1997.

Harbeson, John, and Beaux-Arts Institute of America. *The Study of Architectural Design*. New York: Pencil Points Press, 1927.

Hewitt, Mark Alan. *The Architect and the American Country House, 1890–1940*. New Haven: Yale University Library, 1990.

Hooker, Van Dorn. *Only in New Mexico: An Architectural History of the University of New Mexico, 1889–1989*. Albuquerque: University of New Mexico Press, 2000.

Kelbaugh, Douglas. *Common Place: Toward Neighborhood and Regional Design*. Seattle: University of Washington Press, 1997.

McNary, John C. "John Gaw Meem: His Style Development and Residential Architecture Between 1924 and 1940." Master's thesis, University of New Mexico, 1977.

Markovich, Nicholas C., Wolfgang F. E. Preiser, and Fred Strum, eds. *Pueblo Style and Regional Architecture*. New York: Van Nostrand Reinhold, 1990.

Mather, Christine, and Sharon Woods. *Santa Fe Style*. New York: Rizzoli, 1986.

Mazria, Edward. *The Passive Solar Energy Book*. Emmaus, PA: Rodale Books, 1979.

Nabakov, Peter, and Robert Easton. *Native American Architecture*. New York: Oxford University Press, 1989.

Newcomb, Rexford. *The Spanish House for America.* Philadelphia: Lippincott, 1927.

———. *Spanish-Colonial Architecture in the United States.* 1937, rpt. New York: Dover, 1990.

Polyzoides, Stefanos, Roger Sherwood, and James Tice. *Courtyard Housing in Los Angeles.* 1982, rpt. New York: Princeton Architectural Press, 1992.

Rudnick, Lois Palken. *Utopian Vistas: The Mabel Dodge House and the American Counterculture.* Albuquerque: University of New Mexico Press, 1996.

Seth, Laurel, and Sandra Seth. *Adobe! Homes and Interiors of Taos, Santa Fe and the Southwest.* Stamford, CT: Architectural Book Publishing Company, 1988.

Sexton, R. W. *Spanish Influence on American Architecture and Decoration.* New York: Brentanos, 1927.

Sheppard, Carl D. *Creator of the Santa Fe Style: Isaac Hamilton Rapp.* Albuquerque: University of New Mexico Press, 1988.

Spears, Beverly. *American Adobes.* Albuquerque: University of New Mexico Press, 1986.

Taylor, Anne. *Southwestern Ornamentation and Design: The Architecture of John Gaw Meem.* Santa Fe: Sunstone Press, 1989.

Warren, Nancey Hunter. *New Mexico Style.* Santa Fe: Museum of New Mexico Press, 1986.

Weigle, Marta, and Kyle Fiore. *Santa Fe and Taos: The Writer's Era, 1916–1941.* Santa Fe: Ancient City Press, 1986.

Wilson, Chris. *The Myth of Santa Fe: Creating a Modern Regional Tradition.* Albuquerque: University of New Mexico Press, 1997.

Wirth, Nancy Meem, ed. *Box 628: Recollections and Letters, 1940–1944.* Atherton, CA: n.p., 1990.

———, ed. *Chili Club Papers by John Gaw Meem, 1939–1976.* Santa Fe: n.p., 1994.

CREDITS

All color photography by Robert Reck, except the McLane Residence porch photograph by Chris Wilson in chapter 10, and illustrations on p. 113 by James Hart Photography, Santa Fe. George Clayton Pearl (GCP) produced the supplemental diagrams and plans for this publication.

Permission to reproduce designs by John Gaw Meem and materials from the Meem Collection of the John Gaw Meem Archives of Southwestern Architecture, Center for Southwest Research, Zimmerman Library, University of New Mexico, Albuquerque (UNM), given by Nancy Meem Wirth, holder of Meem design trademarks. In addition, she provided images from her personal collections (NMW) for reproduction.

Permission to reproduce images from the Photo Archives, History Museum, Museum of New Mexico, Santa Fe (MNM), granted by archivist Arthur Olivas.

Permission to reproduce images from the State Records Center and Archives, Santa Fe (SRC), granted by Director Sandra Jaramillo, and Senior Archivist José Villegas.

Permission to reproduce photographs by Laura Gilpin from the Meem Collection granted by Courtney DeAngelis, Associate Registrar, Amon Carter Museum, Ft. Worth, TX, which is the administrator of Gilpin copyrights.

Permission to reproduce photographs by Ansel Adams from the Meem Collection granted by Carolyn Cooper, Office Manager, Ansel Adams Publishing Trust, Mill Valley, CA (AAT), which is the administrator of Adams copyrights.

Permission to reproduce photographs by Ernest Knee from the Meem Collection granted by Gene Kuntz, Santa Fe Editions Gallery (SFE), which is the administrator of Knee copyrights.

p. 2. NMW
pp. 5–9. Courtesy Museum of New Mexico, # 23103
p. 10, left. NMW
p. 10, right. SRC # 23706
p. 10, below. SRC # 23708
pp. 11, 14. NMW
pp. 15, 17. UNM
p. 16, left. Courtesy Museum of New Mexico, # 105557
p. 16, right. Courtesy Museum of New Mexico, # 10690

p. 16, below. Courtesy Museum of New Mexico, # 95327
p. 18, below. NMW
p. 18, above. UNM
p. 19, above. UNM
p. 19, below. *American Architect* magazine, November 1934.
p. 21. UNM
p. 22. Historic American Building Survey. Library of Congress, Washington DC, through UNM
p. 25. UNM and AAT
p. 27, below. UNM
p. 26. UNM, © 1979, Amon Carter Museum, Fort Worth, Texas, Bequest of Laura Gilpin
p. 27, above. GCP
p. 28. UNM
p. 31, below. UNM
p. 31, above. GCP
p. 32. UNM and AAT
p. 33. UNM
p. 37. NMW
p. 38, below. SFE
p. 38, above. Courtesy Museum of New Mexico, #19646
p. 39. UNM, © 1979, Amon Carter Museum, Fort Worth, Texas, Bequest of Laura Gilpin

p. 41. Courtesy Museum
  of New Mexico, # 69279
p. 40, below. UNM and AAT
p. 40, above. UNM, © 1979, Amon Carter
  Museum, Fort Worth, Texas,
  Bequest of Laura Gilpin
p. 42, below. Chris Wilson
p. 43. UNM, © 1979, Amon Carter
  Museum, Fort Worth, Texas,
  Bequest of Laura Gilpin
p. 42, above. Historic American Building
  Survey. Library of Congress,
  Washington DC, through UNM
p. 44. SFE
p. 45, right. UNM
p. 45, left. *Architectural Forum*
  magazine, May 1940.
p. 47. NMW
pp. 48–51. UNM
p. 53. UNM
p. 54. NMW, © 1979, Amon Carter
  Museum, Fort Worth, Texas,
  Bequest of Laura Gilpin
pp. 55–57. UNM
p. 59. NMW
p. 62, above. UNM and SFE
p. 62, below. *Architectural Forum*
  magazine, October 1935
p. 63. GCP

p. 64, above left and right. GCP
p. 64, below left and right. UNM
p. 65, UNM
p. 66. UNM
p. 66. UNM
p. 69, above. UNM
p. 70, above. UNM, AAT
p. 70, below. *American Architect*
  magazine, November 1934
p. 77. GCP
p. 80. GCP
p. 87. GCP
p. 88, above. UNM, © 1979, Amon Carter
  Museum, Fort Worth, Texas,
  Bequest of Laura Gilpin
p. 92. GCP
p. 95, left. UNM, © 1979, Amon Carter
  Museum, Fort Worth, Texas,
  Bequest of Laura Gilpin
p. 94, above. GCP
p. 101, above. UNM, © 1979, Amon Carter
  Museum, Fort Worth, Texas,
  Bequest of Laura Gilpin
p. 102, below. UNM
p. 111, above. UNM
p. 114, below. UNM
p. 119, above. GCP
p. 120. UNM
p. 123, above right. UNM, © 1979, Amon

Carter Museum, Fort Worth, Texas,
  Bequest of Laura Gilpin
p. 124. GCP
p. 127. GCP
p. 128, above. UNM
p. 132, above right. UNM
p. 132, middle right. UNM, AAT
p. 132, above left. UNM, AAT
p. 135, left. UNM
p. 135, right. *American Architect*
  magazine, November 1934
p. 136, below. UNM, AAT
p. 136, above. GCP
p. 138. GCP
p. 140. GCP
p. 142. GCP
p. 148, left. GCP
p. 148, above. UNM
p. 152, above. UNM, © 1979, Amon Carter
  Museum, Fort Worth, Texas,
  Bequest of Laura Gilpin
p. 157, above left. NMW
p. 158, above. GCP
p. 163. NMW, SFE
p. 164. NMW, SFE

INDEX

(Page numbers in italics indicate illustrations.)